10-18-2001 Birmingham, Alabama

Ray

Thank you for all you did at Normandy and in WWII. I have enjoy so much your stories. We are so glad you and Diane come to Alabama. Hope you enjoy this book I got at the National D-Day Museum in New Orleans.

Best regard Fred Sellers

"Now You Know"

Reactions after Seeing
Saving Private Ryan

COMPILED BY AMERICA ONLINE AND DREAMWORKS

Introduction by
Steve Case

Edited by
Jesse Kornbluth and Linda Sunshine

NEWMARKET PRESS • NEW YORK

America Online and DreamWorks are donating
all royalties and earnings from this book to:
The National D-Day Museum
923 Magazine Street
New Orleans, LA 70130
Toll-free: 1-877-813-DDAY (3329)
Web site: www.ddaymuseum.org

Reproduction of Robert Niland letter shown on page 118, courtesy of Art and
Photographic Services, University at Buffalo (State University of New York), and the
Niland family.

Poem on page 63 copyright © 1998 M. Bardine. Reprinted by permission of the author.

All messages are reprinted by permission of the authors — all America Online
members — and America Online which owns the copyright in the compilation and
arrangement of the messages. The e-mail addresses of the authors have been omitted
herein to protect their privacy. Historical photographs are reprinted by permission of
the donors, and credited within.

 Published by Newmarket Press, New York.

First Edition

10 9 8 7 6 5 4 3 2 1

ISBN: 1-55704-384-1 (hardcover)

Library of Congress Cataloging-in-Publication Data is available on request.

This book is published simultaneously in the United States and Canada.

Quantity Purchases: Companies, professional groups, clubs, and other organizations
may qualify for special terms when ordering quantities of this title. For information,
write Special Sales, Newmarket Press, 18 East 48th Street, New York, NY 10017,
call (212) 832-3575, or fax (212) 832-3629.

Designed by Timothy Shaner

Manufactured in the United States of America.

*Photo right: Lieutenant JG William Robert McCown (back row, first on left),
U.S. Navy, South Pacific, circa 1944. Courtesy of Edna McCown.*

Contents

Photo left: Frances and Sergeant George Datres, Spruce Creek, Pennsylvania, 1943. Courtesy of Illene Shaner.

Tom Hagen – my Uncle –

Introduction

Most major films get so much pre-release media coverage that by the time they reach theaters you feel as if you've already seen them. Steven Spielberg wanted *Saving Private Ryan* to be different. He wanted it to be a pure and unexpected emotional experience, unaffected by pre-release publicity. So for most of America, Spielberg's film was very much like D-Day itself — towering, dramatic, and a near-total surprise.

At America Online, we knew in advance that Spielberg had a big new movie coming out. But no one at AOL knew just how powerful it was until a picture-and-text book, *Saving Private Ryan: The Men, The Mission, The Movie*, was delivered to us about ten days before the film opened.

Looking at the pictures taken from the film was like stepping back into time behind a photographer's lens on D-Day. There was one picture of a soldier — an actor — being literally blown off his feet. The image was so powerful and so real that it gave you the chills to look at it.

From the moment we got that book, it was clear that *Saving Private Ryan* wasn't going to be just a film — it was going to be a profound and personal experience for millions of Americans. More important, it was clear that watching it would be only part of that experience. Afterward, people were going to want to discuss it.

That's where we knew AOL could play an important role.

Photo left: Service Company, 4th Infantry Regiment, Fort Benning, Georgia, 1944.
Courtesy of John Nye.

Every day, millions of AOL members come online to meet and talk, to exchange information and make friends, to laugh and yell and debate and cajole.

That daily dialogue has grown to astonishing proportions. On a typical day, AOL members now exchange nearly 50 million individual e-mails and a whopping 400 million Instant Messages. They take part in so many chat rooms and message boards that we need a small army of 14,000 volunteers just to keep track.

The day that *Saving Private Ryan* opened, we launched a special section of AOL devoted to the movie. Created by Jesse Kornbluth, AOL's Editorial Director of Channel Programming, the *Saving Private Ryan* area had links to reviews of the film, to historical accounts of D-Day, and to books about World War II. But the most significant link was to a message board about the film — and about that war.

"What soldiers have seen, others cannot imagine," was the introduction at the top of that message board. "*Saving Private Ryan* may spark an outpouring of painful, moving memories about war. We invite you to share them here."

And share our members did. That first weekend, you could visit that message board, note the number of messages posted there, go away and immediately return — and find a hundred new messages. All weekend, the messages came like that: in waves. You could almost picture our members stumbling out of the theaters and, with their eyes still damp and their emotions still raw, logging on to AOL to share their memories and feelings.

These messages were stunning in their intimacy. Children
of veterans wrote to say how sad they were that their fathers
had never spoken of the war — but now they understood why.
Other children of veterans wrote to say they had seen the film
with their fathers and had wept together. Some wrote to
thank veterans for heroism on a scale they could hardly
imagine, to wonder if today's young men could rise to such a
challenge, or to ask if war could ever be stopped.

Five thousand messages, ten thousand, fifteen thousand.
Within days, the *Saving Private Ryan* message board had
become the center of a national conversation about this film
and about war in general. Newspapers wrote about this
phenomenon and what AOL members were sharing. That
public exposure led to even more messages — and to this book.

In the end, about 30,000 AOL members posted their
thoughts and opinions, their memories and emotions on the
Saving Private Ryan message board. We've chosen a
representative sampling of their posts here. To read them in
one sitting is an intense and emotional experience.

I hope you will be as moved by the power and insight of
what our members wrote as I was. And I also hope you will
share my excitement about how they have used our extraordinary interactive medium to share, to understand, and to grow.
For both reasons, I'm immensely proud of this book and very
grateful to the AOL members who are its true authors.

— Steve Case
Chairman and CEO, America Online
February, 1999

Part One

"Now You Know . . ."

Overleaf photo: Lieutenant Commander Emmett F. Gebauer, U.S. Navy, Guadalcanal.
Courtesy of Jenine Davison.

Now you know . . .

My grandfather, who is a 72-year-old naval veteran of WWII, never really talked about his experience during the war. At the age of 17, he left a poverty-stricken home and set out to join the Navy because he felt like it was his only way out and, more importantly, his duty. During rare moments, he would talk about his life in the Navy and what it brought to him.

It wasn't until I was almost 17 years old that he began to open up about the things he saw and how they made him feel. After he realized that we would listen, it was like a dam had broken. He talked for hours one Sunday afternoon, and what he told us made our lives seem so very easy, to say the least. The horrors he suffered all the long months he served have made him a harder human being. The lessons he learned have made him wise beyond his years. And the friendships he formed and lost have made him care more about those who are important to him and make it harder for him to let go.

Last weekend, we saw "Saving Private Ryan" together, the whole family. His face wore a look of indifference and doubt. But in the end, he cried. I have never seen my grandfather cry, but on that day he did. We left the movie theater and walked in the rain to our cars and the tears still fell. He had only one comment, "Now you know how it really was for me. . . ."

He has yet to say anything more. The wounds are finally healing for him after holding the hurt in for so many years. With time, he may be able to move on, but letting go of our past means we let go of what makes us who we are. I realize that there may be so many others out there who feel the same way as my grandfather. Thank you for what you did and the manner in which you did it. Words cannot express the grateful thanks that so many Americans feel. And Grandpa, thank you for opening up and sharing that moment of your life. . . . May you remember only good and let the bad slip away . . . then again, so might you all.

This movie caused my grandpa pain

My grandpa went to see "Saving Private Ryan," and it moved him deeply. He was in World War II in the 29th division and 175th infantry. He was also a POW.

He was in total shock because the movie brought back many horrible memories of the war. He said that the movie was very close to the "real thing." After seeing it, he cried for three days straight. I think that the movie was good, but now I know how bad it really was in World War II.

And from the same member, posted at a later date . . .

When I saw my Grandpa last night, I gave him a huge hug and said, "That hug is from America, Grandpa. You are a true hero and America thanks you for being such a brave man in World War II."

He started to cry and said, "I gave America all I had in me and I'm happy I did."

Later that night he asked me where I had gotten the idea of him being a "true hero" and I told him about the post I made on this message board and the response that I got from it and he told me to tell all of you thanks for caring and he will never forget you all and that he will keep you in his prayers.

My father at "Bloody Omaha"

I went to see "Pvt. Ryan" a few days ago. I usually cry when I see movies that touch me personally. For some reason, I did not. I think I was looking at it from a historical perspective. Subconsciously I think I was looking for my dad!

My dad was a Navy signalman who was on the third row of landing craft at Omaha Beach on June 6th. For many years he could never talk to anyone (except my mother) about that day. I was grown before he told me what happened, and then it was only in small detail.

As the years went by and the pain lessened, he told me how he was a crewman on an LCI. The boat was to go in to the beach, drop its cargo of men, then return to the main ship offshore for more troops. He saw the first row of landing craft drop its men, but they were ripped to pieces or drowned and never even made it out of the water.

Dad was on a boat in the third row. By the time he got to the beach, the water was already littered with bodies and the sea was red with blood. Dad's boat was able to unload, leave the beach, and return a second time with more men.

The second time he was not as lucky. One of the crew was hit, his head landing on the deck. Dad was ordered to kick the poor soldier's head off into the water. Then the whole boat was blown out from under him. Dad made it to shore and found cover at the foot of the beach cliff. The pillbox was above him. And there he stayed. He said it was the saddest place on earth.

I watched the movie intensely, trying to put myself in Dad's boots. I really found myself there, and I think now that I understand better why he had such a hard time talking about Omaha Beach.

After the movie, I made a point to call him. I wanted to warn him: "Don't go." It was too late. He had seen it — and had cried through the first 30 minutes. He had not been told about the graphic depiction of the landing. There were many other veterans in the audience who also were ill prepared for what they were about to see. I truly believe that the producers should have printed a "warning label."

But I don't want to imply that it was wrong to have such a vivid portrayal of war. In fact, I must admit that in some ways it might be a good thing. It might put to rest some of the suppressed memories some vets have carried for over 50 years.

I expect this movie to win all kinds of awards. It is deserving. Wouldn't it be wonderful if all the vets could get awards too?

A member responds to "My father at 'Bloody Omaha'"

I too have a father who was in the war. My dad was on Omaha Beach on Day Two. While watching the movie, I was moved. I then spoke to my dad and when he told me he was there the day after what we saw at the movie, I was in a state of shock.

Unlike other fathers, mine never shared the bad times of war. It was too painful. Now that he has seen the movie and 50 years have passed, he can deal with talking about it.

Post-traumatic stress

My dad suffered post-traumatic stress from WWII also — although he called it "shell shock." It made him mean and overly emotional.

I saw the movie "Patton" a long time ago. The scene where Patton slapped the shell-shocked soldier made me think of my dad. After that, I always thought of my dad as a coward. After seeing "Saving Private Ryan," I can understand why he was affected this way. I couldn't possibly have imagined how horrible the war was until now. He died two years ago. I wish I could tell him I was sorry.

My father never talks

My father served in Europe from D-Day to the Battle of the Bulge, and who knows after that. He never talked about the war. When I asked him questions, he would just say that he took a lot of lives and that's all I need to know. I did learn that he was wounded three times, was a sergeant, and all the men under him died during the war, except one.

As children, our family once drove to his surviving buddy's home and stayed for the week. I overheard my father talking to his army buddy about the Battle of the Bulge. He spoke about the time when he was firing the machine gun that was attached to the back of the jeep his buddy drove until the gun began to melt from all the firing. He must have seen a great deal of horror.

My father drank every night. He never played with his children or had father-son talks. When I was a child, I always wondered what was wrong with him. As I got older I began to understand how damaged he was. Today, I am a clinical social worker. I have treated many clients with post-traumatic stress disorder. I understand now that he can't get close to anyone, as he has lost his ability to do so. The war cost him not only his army friends, but also his ability to have a close family relationship.

My father is still alive. He still drinks. He is still alone. He is the living dead.

The bonds of silence

They came back wanting to forget. They grew up with the Depression, and walked into the worst maelstrom imaginable that war and technology could devise.

Taciturn, stoical, believing that it was better to stuff feelings — grin and bear it, "We all got troubles of our own, pal" — they returned from hell and made America prosper as we never had before.

Unable to break the bonds that silence wrought, when their sons were called upon to fight in Southeast Asia, they readied the country for their last war. They called for loyalty, obedience to authority, and sacrifice. What we needed were thoughtful questions of authority and respectful answers.

Perhaps if they could have unburdened themselves in the "Leave it to Beaver" era, Vietnam would have been a non-starter.

I grew up with WWII and the Holocaust being discussed often. When I was old enough to understand — perhaps 8 or 10 — it was only 14 years after D-Day.

I worshipped the heroism and action of those giants. My dad enlisted on June 6, 1944, his 17th birthday.

I just wish they could have talked more, felt and expressed more. I mourn for the huge losses of WWII. Thirty million dead — just try to think of it! What carnage, what waste. Pain rippling out through lives and generations. Pray for peace.

Spielberg tried to use the medium to make magic: to put us there, on the other side of the screen. He didn't use the tricks of the trade for cheap entertainment, but to help us transcend what we know of our lives, to be in some faint way with those boys who could never be prepared for what they had to face, and who gave everything so early, so young in life, they couldn't know fully the huge gift they gave.

Western Union

I was 15 at the time of D-Day and had been a camp follower with my mother from camp to camp until my father went overseas. The scene of the priest and the Army officer coming up the road brought back vivid memories of the Western Union messenger in his company uniform pedaling his bicycle by our house to deliver the "Regret to inform you" telegrams to our friends and neighbors. Every male member of our family for three generations has served in the armed forces, and we have been fortunate not to have received one of these messages.

Even now at the age of 70, my thoughts and prayers were with Mrs. Ryan as that car made the long journey up the drive.

A young man's opinion

I'll be twenty-one in less than a month. I know what this means, too. I'm young. I have no idea what war is really like. I wasn't there. I've heard the stories, but I've never had to experience the blood washing ashore on the beach or the sound of a bullet whizzing by my head. I haven't seen any combat and I couldn't imagine myself firing a gun or driving a knife in another human being.

In other words, I don't know what I'm talking about.

But both of my grandfathers did fight in the Second World War. My paternal grandfather was a medic in the Navy, my maternal grandfather a gunnery sergeant in the marines.

When I saw "Saving Private Ryan," the thoughts that rang through my head the entire time were that I knew people who did these things. People I loved, people whose blood I carry in me, fought in these battles. For the first time, the stories I've heard all my life became real. And I am humbled.

Casualties on Omaha Beach on D-Day

I have seen the cemetery — it is enormous. The predominant burials are from casualties of June 6th. However, there are many for June 5th! (Pre-invasion drop?) And of course many for the 7th.

My father was on Omaha Beach. He was a Navy signalman who made it in as a crewman on an LCI. His boat was blown up, but he survived and made it to shore. Since he was unattached to a unit command, he had to stay there for a few days. He went to the top of the cliffs several times to help with and watch the burials.

He said bodies were stacked so high! One dog tag was placed with the soldier who was lovingly placed in a canvas bag. Each was buried in a single grave. A temporary marker was placed at his head and the other dog tag was put there until an accounting of the burial was made.

Talk to them about WWII while they're here. . . .

My Dad was a WWII veteran, and just passed away July 10, 1998, of cancer. Although I thought I had asked him most everything I could think of, after seeing "Saving Private Ryan" I realized there was much, much more I should have asked.

Like: "What type of 'action' did you see?" "What were your fears, and what was it like?" "Did you ever see your friends killed?" "Did you ever have to kill others?" "Did you think you'd never come home?" "Were you aware of the 'overall' problems you were combating, or did you just complete little missions, not really seeing the bigger picture?"

If you still have your relatives/loved ones who fought, take the time to thank them and to let them know it's important to those of us who will remain.

My Dad never talked about the war much, which tells me what a great man he was, very humble, and expecting no special recognition for all he had done to keep me free. Whenever I did ask him anything, he would always discount it as "just doing his part towards what needed to be done for our great country, and to keep us free." Thanks, Dad, for more than being a great Dad, but for helping the rest of us live in peace.

Thanks, Uncle Lawson

My uncle was killed on Omaha Beach on June 6, 1944. Hey, Uncle Lawson, I'm an Army officer now, too — and though I never met you, I will never forget how frightened you must have been, how you went anyway, and how you had your life stolen from you by Germans early in the morning. Thank you! I will meet you someday and catch up.

Understanding my father

My Dad hit a beach in WWII. He was wounded and lay on the beach for 16 hours. That event changed his life; the pain stayed with him all his life. Seeing this movie brought me close to my father for the first time. I understand what I couldn't before now. I don't think I could have survived what he went through.

He received a Purple Heart, we received a tortured soul. I know if he had it to do again, my father would take that beach and that bullet again. I love him and I am very proud of him and hope that no other person has to go through such horrors again.

I understand now

I am a 37 year-old daughter of a WWII vet. My father, as well as 3 of his brothers, served at the same time. (They were 4 of 10 brothers.) Amazingly, they all came home. My dad would never discuss the war.

I remember very clearly the day I took his Purple Heart and Bronze Star to kindergarten for "show and tell." I didn't put them away after school, and when he came home from work that day and saw them out, he was furious. "Don't you ever take those out of the house again! I did a lot of things over there that I'm not too proud of. Don't go around showing those off," he told me.

I was too little to understand those words at the time, but I never forgot them. We never did discuss the war again, but I always wondered what it meant to him. When he became ill with cancer, he asked my sister to give those two medals to his grandsons to remember him by. His Army uniform still hangs in a garment bag in my mother's closet. I guess it meant something he didn't know how to put into words.

I think WWII left a whole generation of men who were damaged somehow. Back in the 40s it wasn't masculine to discuss your feelings — or wear your heart on your sleeve, as my father would say. He would never have considered going to a support group, even if there were such a thing then. I think it probably came out in different ways, like alcoholism for some, physical abuse, or depressed silence, for those like mine.

The one thing I do remember is that he never talked about it. He was on the beach that day. Now I finally understand why.

The people of Normandy remember

The summer of 1994 marked the 50th anniversary of the invasion of Normandy. There was no better time for me to go there to try to find the place where my father was killed. My family knew almost nothing about the seven days that he survived after landing at Omaha Beach on July 24th. On August 1, two days before I was born, he was killed on a hill overlooking the village of Percy in lower Normandy.

My arrival in Percy was not anticipated by any of its citizens. Once my presence became known, I became the benefactor of numerous acts of kindness and generosity. My new French friends possess a deep and sincere appreciation for the sacrifices we made on their behalf.

That summer, each town in Normandy held its own commemoration services on the anniversary of its individual liberation. These took place far from the landing beaches and media attention. They were very personal affairs because they brought back somber memories of destruction and personal loss. Percy had lost 46 of its own people in the summer of 1944. For a town so small, that was indeed a significant number of casualties. The town itself was almost completely destroyed.

As the only American in town on this occasion, I became the de facto representative of those who gave their lives along with my father. This was an honor I did not personally deserve but I was proud to accept in their memory.

On July 31st, a service was held in the restored church of St. Jean Baptiste. I was asked to be in the procession side by side with the French veterans. We proceeded into the church followed by all the citizens of the town. There was music, poetry, and a memorial sermon that, because of my very limited understanding of the language, was mostly lost on me. Following the service everyone gathered outside around a modest monument to their lost citizens to hear a brief speech by their mayor, Dr. Michel Loreille.

Dr. Loreille called upon all who were present to never forget those young Americans who left their homes never to return again. The mayor interrupted his speech to ask me to come forward. He introduced me to all who were present, explaining that I had, in his words, come in my father's footsteps to remember him at this special time.

When the speech was over, the town's fire brigade band played our national anthem. Being so far from home and feeling the embrace of so many strangers touched me very deeply.

After the services concluded, everyone retired to a large hall for refreshments and informal greetings. One man who approached me with tears in his eyes simply said, "Thank you for your father." I will never forget the nine days I spent with the grateful people of Normandy. It was gratifying to know that my father's sacrifice meant so much to the good people of this little town. I remain in contact with several of my new French friends. I hope to someday accept the many invitations to return to Percy with my family.

Army combat medic

I spent two tours in Vietnam, and was wounded five times. I can honestly say the combat medics are the bravest, most honorable men I ever met!

I couldn't count the times our medic risked his life to save ours. My second greatest gift from 'Nam was that my medic made it home alive!

A father lost . . . a father found . . .

My father was killed in World War II in 1945 when I was only 18 months old. His plane was shot down by a Japanese warship in the Pacific, and although I had a few snapshots and one treasured portrait of him in his flying uniform, I really never knew this man who helped bring me into the world. He was an idealized, almost mythic figure to me, and I accepted, as children do, the fact that I had no father.

My mother remarried in 1950, and my stepfather, who had been in the Navy at Pearl Harbor when it was bombed, was now in the Army. He was stationed in Germany starting in 1953, and there I saw, at the impressionable age of 10 years, bombed-out cities and people living in ruins. The war became real to me.

My stepfather had lost a brother in the D-Day invasion, so he very much wanted to go the cemetery at Omaha Beach to find his grave. We went, and to this day I can remember the sights, sounds, and feelings that overwhelmed me as we walked. I had seen war pictures and knew of the terrible battle that occurred during the invasion, but that day it was a silent, peaceful place . . . clear blue sky with a gentle breeze off the water. The rows and rows and rows of white crosses went on forever in every direction — I was stunned by that sight more than any pictures of the battle. It seemed there was now an army of white crosses forever guarding this coastline of France from any assaults on freedom ever again.

More than any ruins or museums or pictures I have ever seen, that sight had the greatest impact of the losses of lives that occurred — not just at that spot, but during that whole, hellish war. I grew up with the greatest respect for my father and stepfather and all those men like them who went through such unimaginable horrors.

Thirty-five years later my husband and I went to Hawaii, and I had learned of the Punchbowl Cemetery in Honolulu and wanted to go there. It, too, seemed to be almost otherworldly in beauty and peace, and there was a simple but majestic monument to the servicemen who died in the Pacific during WWII. I was shaking with emotion as I saw the large columns with names engraved on them. Suddenly I found myself looking at my father's name and at that sight, there overlooking the Pacific where he died, I broke down and wept and wept for the father I had found at last. He had lived, and died so very young, but he was remembered.

"Saving Private Ryan" reminds us we must NEVER stop remembering them all and what they went through for all of us.

Response to: A father lost . . . a father found . . .

I'm sorry you never knew your dad. But now, perhaps, you know how brave he was. And that others recognize his sacrifice. My dad made it out alive. He, too, was just a kid, when he crawled up on that red sand. An innocent boy who lived a lifetime of horror in just a few months. An angel sat upon his shoulder and carried him through two more major battles in France.

He came back home, met and married my Mom, and went on to a 30-year career in the Air Force. I remember seeing the shrapnel wounds on his old head (he wore a military crew cut). I never asked why they were there. We all lived our idyllic existence, totally unaware of what he had gone through.

He didn't have the support groups that Vietnam Vets have now . . . he just went on and lived his life and put those vicious memories away somewhere. I'm sure they revisited him at times when he least expected. He didn't whine or complain, my dad. It pains me to know what horrors were swirling around in his battle-scarred head.

When I was a teenager, I remember thinking how clueless he was. After this movie, I can tell you: He is more man than anybody I know. He is 75 now, gray, and has grown smaller, now, and he totters. It is hard to imagine him, young, strong, and scared to death as he belly-crawled through the gore.

He has never talked about this experience in his life, but

now I feel compelled to sit down with him and prod him.
Gently, though, for I don't want to disturb the bad place inside
him where the beastly sights, sounds, and smell lurk. I will love
and honor my Dad, and in doing this, your Dad is honored.

God bless you and your family. You all paid a terrible price,
but you can be proud of your Dad. I'm glad you found him and
I know he felt your presence. I'm 44, and I thought I was pretty
seasoned — how wrong I was. I'm still learning about life and
death on this earth of ours, and the ghosts that traverse it.

Now I understand

My uncle never talked about the war. I had heard that during the
war he had been one of the soldiers who parachuted into
Germany and helped liberate the camps. He was taken prisoner by a
young German soldier, and ultimately had to kill him to get away.

One of the things that made this especially bad was that my uncle's
family had emigrated to the U.S. from Prussia. I know now why he
never talked about it. I was shaking when I left the movie. I can't begin
to imagine how it felt to live with the memories of the reality.

Freedom is not free

I am one of the 2.5 million old soldiers who retired from the U.S. military. The movie brought me back to a lonely dark night in the platoon bunker facing a real enemy who has yet to agree to sign a peace treaty, that being the North Korean Army. We received intelligence that there was a movement of a platoon of the North Korean Army south of the North/South border. Although not the most forward position, it was established that this unit had bypassed the two forward battalions, and we were the last lines of defense.

As the night passed and we started out into the pitch darkness, a song started quietly among the other bunkers. The song kept coming and coming down the line until the whole camp was singing it, be it Republic of Korea Army or U.S. Army personnel. The song was "Silent Night," for it was two nights before Christmas.

My grandfather was at Omaha

My grandfather was on the first wave into Omaha beach, and he made it through. When I was watching "Saving Private Ryan," I kept placing him in that situation, and at that moment I found a new respect for my grandfather. He literally went through hell and risked his life for his country.

He has told me many stories about the blood and carnage. I tried to picture it, but I could have never done it the way the movie did. I love my grandfather and every time I think about him going through that I shiver because I know that if one bullet had hit him, I might never have been here to see this movie or write this post.

Thoughts of a soldier

I always thought I was prepared to go to war. After seeing the film I am not so sure. I was an infantryman (like the soldiers storming the beach), and I am now a cavalry scout. When you are training, you don't think about dying or about the guy next to you dying, you just do your job.

I believe in what I do. That might make me old fashioned, but that is fine with me. For at least four generations my family has served in the military, and I stand proud to carry on the tradition.

I believe that the movie should stand as a reminder to everyone just how horrible war can be, so that people like me never have to do our job.

Saw the movie with my dad

I loved the movie and was so proud to sit beside my 78-year-old dad who served in World War II. He was an airplane mechanic (my Mom also) and did not see combat (thank God), but I'm sure he heard many stories of the brutality and horror that other young men his age had to face.

During the movie my father repeated to me several times, "As gruesome as these scenes are, it is not even close to what these men had to face." At the end he simply said, "Times ten!"

My grandfather . . .

I took my grandfather to see this movie because he saw the previews to it and he said he wanted to see it. I have never seen my grandfather cry like he did yesterday when he came out of that theater. He said it was so close to the real thing that he couldn't have imagined it better.

My uncle was there

When I saw "Private Ryan," I too was moved. You see, my uncle was there too. He'd fought across Africa, Sicily, and then he was at Omaha, in the first wave as the commander of a DD Sherman.

His was one of the very few tanks to actually make it to the beach, and although he got there, they didn't get far, as the tank promptly got stuck in the mud. They dueled a few 88s, got hit by an 88 round that went right through the engine compartment (and the engine) without exploding, and basically shot up all their ammo at pillboxes and machine gun positions, until they were hit again and forced to abandon the tank. He spent the rest of the day in a shell hole, aiding the medics.

But the sights and sounds of D-Day and Omaha Beach didn't really faze him that much. He'd been fighting too long, and these sorts of sights were common to him by then. He always said that it bothered him that he'd become used to such things, but the mind does what it has to do to survive.

He said the real nightmares didn't begin until he began liberating concentration camps.

He always said that if he did nothing else in life, then he hoped what he'd done with his time in the Army made the world a better place. I think he did. Thanks, Uncle C. . . . My world is better because of men like you. . . .

My father at Normandy

My father, after years of silence, revealed to us that his ship was there. I couldn't believe it! I am 47 years old, and I wondered why he didn't tell us.

They were in charge of the transportation to the beach. He stayed on the ship and couldn't believe what he saw through binoculars on the beach. After this movie, I saw the ships out there and thought, "Dad, I'm glad you are still with us, and I'm glad you were on a ship and not on the beach."

I didn't want to see this movie. I hate war films. I'm glad I did, and have encouraged my teenagers (16 & 19) to see it too. After all, they should have some idea why Grandpa couldn't speak of it after all these years and maybe even why their mother protested the war in the 60s.

I knew what was coming

I started crying in the first three minutes. I knew what was coming. I knew our history. I cried through the rest of the movie. I am crying now. I am 62 years old and I am not ashamed to admit I am crying. How do you say "thank you" to all those "dogfaces," "fly boys," "jarheads," and "swamp jockeys" who saved the whole world and our freedom in those four years? This movie goes a long way to the answer.

Now I understand

My grandfather was in D-Day, and my own mother didn't know about it for a long while — in fact, up to the 50th anniversary — that he was there. He didn't want to remember what happened when he hit that beach, or tell anyone else. People like my grandfather have kept our country from having to salute someone else's flag.

Normandy

I lost my dad to cancer almost one year ago. He was in World War II. I know he was with me throughout this movie and saying: "This is what it was like for me. But I was able to come home . . . then have you. . . ."

My father at Normandy

My dad is 73 and was a 20mm gun operator on the USS McCook off Omaha Beach at Normandy. He spoke little of the carnage he saw from his GQ station that day. He never wanted us to know. This movie revealed what he has kept inside all these years.

My God, what bravery! I did not think it was possible to love and respect my father any more than I had, but this movie has shed new light on my father and why he is the kind of man he is. Thank you, dad, and all others who have fought and died for our country so I can live the good life. I love you, dad.

Part Two

"I Understand My Father Now"

Overleaf photo: Major John Truell, U.S. Air Force, South Pacific.
Courtesy of Donald Arganbright.

I understand my father now

My father was in the Navy during WWII and was involved in the battle of Normandy. During my childhood I only remember him being an alcoholic, abusing me and 2 of my brothers. But what stands out more are the many times Dad would wake up in a cold sweat shaking and crying. He used to tell us about the war but wouldn't talk about Normandy. Even when he abused us, my heart broke every time I saw my dad cry, and I wished I could help him feel better. He never let me comfort him — that also made me sad.

After seeing the movie "Saving Private Ryan" today, I was left shaking and finally understood the anguish my dad and all those men went through, and now, as I look to the Heavens, tears running down my face, I say, Dear Dad, I forgive you, and Now I Understand and I'm sorry it took me 37 years to do it.

God Bless All Of You Who Have Fought For This Country.
I Love You, Dad
Your Daughter

Daddy . . . thank you

I used to get frustrated when I would ask you questions about being in WWII. I knew you lied about your age and joined the Navy, and I knew you were in some major conflict, and once I saw you looking through a battered metal box with purple ribbon and some medals in it. But you never, never, never would talk about it. Now I know. I wish I'd known before you died a year ago this month. I wish I had known when they played taps and fired the 21-gun salute. I wish I had known. But now I do know . . . thank you . . . and it's OK that you didn't talk about it. Thank you, Steven Spielberg, for showing me my dad, when I've waited 22 years to see.

Why visit a rerun?

I asked my father if he planned to view SPR to which he replied, "Why? Been there, done that, I don't need to view or be reminded of what took place. I'm still trying to forget that battle. I lost too many friends."

As a young man I viewed the movie "Patton" with him and I remember how he left to go to the men's room several times, returning each time with tears in his eyes. Today I realize the courage he displayed back then merely by attending that movie. SPR was all the more real. He didn't need to view more real — he'd been there to experience it. The film performed a great service to all those who served. It makes us realize that freedom sometimes requires the ultimate sacrifice. Too often we take for granted the shade the tree of Liberty provides to us when so many young brave soldiers continue to give their blood to feed it. I'm very grateful for that young lieutenant who went back for my dad, found him unconscious, his feet frozen, in that frozen fox hole, and hauled his butt out of Battle of the Bulge. For if he hadn't done so, neither I nor his six grandchildren would be here.

Response to: Why visit a rerun?

I can understand why your father may want to forget that battle, but it is imperative that the rest of us don't forget. We can't forget the men that fought and died there. We can't forget the men who came home wounded physically and mentally. If it takes a movie like "Saving Private Ryan" to wake up a whole generation to the atrocities of war, then so be it.

We all need to "earn it" like Private Ryan was asked to do. The soldiers of WWII sacrificed everything for us — the future generations. Are we earning that sacrifice? Are we living lives that are worthy of that sacrifice? That is a question we all have to ask ourselves and live with every day.

Now I know . . .

Now I know what my quiet and unassuming father went through in his youth. A first lieutenant in Normandy at age 22, he received a Silver Star for his actions against an SS Panzer unit while defending a bridge. Of his company of 120 men only 40 survived.

This movie has struck a chord so close to home I am having trouble typing.

I am proud to be his son.

I finally "get" it

After seeing "Saving Private Ryan," I finally have a much better understanding of why my husband will not talk about his experiences in Vietnam and why my father will also not talk about his experiences during WWII. My husband only says, "It's over," and my dad always told us, "I got through it, now drop the subject."

I cannot imagine being an 18-year-old marine (as was my father) and having to witness the horrors that he did. I have a new respect for all the veterans after seeing this movie — one that I can understand just a little bit better, and I thank them for the rest of our lives.

For my father

I felt a great personal need to see "Saving Private Ryan." My father was in the second wave of soldiers on Omaha Beach. He never really talked about WWII, and when I saw this movie I understood why. How could he? He was also shot on that beach but survived and went on to the Battle of the Bulge. My Dad has been dead for 10 years but he did instill a healthy respect in me regarding all veterans of all wars. Later in life he joined the VFW and was a commander there. His motto was, "Respect the dead by helping the living."

This movie has had a profound effect on me. It has been on my mind since I saw it and I think that is a good thing. A couple of my brothers also fought in Vietnam; the younger said he couldn't see this film, as it would be too painful. He also said movies could not capture the "smell of war." I feel this is a movie that needed to be made, and I'm thankful to all involved for having the courage and personal stamina to do it. War is not healthy for children and other living things — remember that from the '60s. We can never know what our vets went through; this film gives us a glance at that.

My reasons on why this movie should be watched

This movie should be seen by everyone age 16 and up. And there is good reason why.

I am the 21-year-old son of a 32-year army veteran. I cannot pretend to truly understand what war and combat is like, but I feel that I am wise enough to realize that it is not anything a sane man would wish to experience.

"Saving Private Ryan" helps convey that message to people who might not truly understand it. I went to this movie with several friends after seeing it once with my father. I had difficulty viewing it a second time. As the trailers and previews ran, there was some noise in the audience and a fair amount of catcalls and giggling. The giggling continued even through the opening of the movie, with the elderly Ryan and his family. The giggling soon stopped when the film took us to Normandy on June 6th.

My generation has been desensitized to violence. We speak of guns and explosions and watch them with such disinterest and detachment. "Saving Private Ryan" changes that. All my friends, the young ladies and young men both, were struck with the intensity and casual horror of the opening invasion scenes. It was unlike anything we'd ever witnessed before, and as a group, we later decided it was a good thing we saw it. After all, we are the age of people who will be the flesh of the Armed Forces, or the people who may vote to use those forces.

Daughter of veteran

I didn't understand why my dad never spoke about his experiences in WWII. He died peacefully in his bed at home on Jan. 6, 1997, holding my hand. I was lucky to have had the opportunity to kiss him goodbye and tell him how much I loved him. The day before he died I sat on his bed and asked him to tell me how he was feeling, specifically, I asked him if he was afraid to die. He looked at me and said, "What is there to be afraid of?"

Although he knew he was dying of terminal cancer, he did not choose to share any fear with me. I have a much better understanding of his bravery and his values after seeing "Saving Private Ryan."

I felt so many emotions during the movie — fear, panic, distrust, anger, disappointment, horror, pain, love, emptiness, happiness, compassion, confusion, responsibility, guilt, etc. The problems that I have faced in my 51 years seem totally insignificant after seeing this movie. I wish Dad were here now so I could tell him how much I appreciate his efforts to insure my freedom. I will visit his gravesite in Arlington National Cemetery and thank him and all the others who fought for future generations.

It made me cry

My father-in-law participated in D-day, landing on Omaha Beach. After he saw the movie, he called each of his children to tell them that all the answers to what it was like were in the movie. My husband and I went, knowing that the opening scenes would be brutal. They certainly were. I could appreciate, for the first time, the fear of the unknown, the panic of nowhere to go, and the final irrational decisions to move because there was no alternative.

As the band's journey began, my thoughts shifted to my own father, now deceased, and I began to realize my misconceptions that, somehow, a war fought on domestic lands would be simpler. Seeing the towns reduced to rubble (not what I had imagined them to be) made what little information my father had shared comprehensible for the first time. But why was I crying as I walked out of the movie?

Because Tom Hanks's character had to believe that his life and the lives of his men were worth the sacrifice. That perhaps he was saving the life of a man who would go on to do something amazing, important, and valuable to the entire human race. But did Private Ryan go on to do that? The movie didn't say, and because it didn't, we could assume that, no, he didn't. Instead, what did he do? He was a "good man." He raised his family and they grew to have their own families. It was then that I realized that the children of those warriors were, for many of them, their contributions to mankind. That the act of coming home, having a family, and giving them all the benefits they could achieve was how they "earned it." My father survived the war and came home. He did not invent the light bulb. He did not do anything miraculous, except live with his memories of the war, silently, and raise a family to the best of his ability. To that end, I am part of the bargain that was made. I am the outcome of the sacrifice. Have I "earned it"?

Dying

My father never told me about his WWII experiences until he was 4 days from death from cancer in 1992. He explained, in the same detail as "Saving Private Ryan," the terrible truth about war and his experience in the Pacific theater.

After seeing the movie, I know why he never wanted me to go to Vietnam.

I love you, Dad.

A grandchild's impression

My grandfather always told short stories about fighting in France during WWII, but I thought he was just making them up. Teenagers today have no idea of what it is like to be in war and therefore dismiss them as stupid stories. After seeing this movie, I understand what my grandfather was always trying to tell me. War is not glamorous or cool; it is a terrible experience and people should be grateful that they did not have to experience it.

I now have enormous respect for my grandfather and all other veterans. They gave their lives to make our country a better place to live. I am a gen-Xer and am ashamed to be associated with some of the people on this board. They make our generation look like a bunch of idiots who don't care about anyone. I would like to see them in war and see how they respond. Our fathers and grandfathers fought and died so we would not have to. We should love and respect them for that. This movie was so powerful and moving. I wasn't crying until the end when the older Private Ryan was standing at the grave. He looked so much like my grandfather that I couldn't help but cry. Who would I be if he had died in that war?

I thanked my dad

I spoke with my dad long distance last weekend after I saw the movie. I talked to him about it and encouraged him to go see it. He declined, saying he couldn't handle it emotionally right now (he's 81 now). This came from a man who served in the Pacific in a non-combatant role. I think that shows just how deep an impact the war had on all who served. I told my dad I was very proud of him and his generation and that I will make sure that my children do not forget the sacrifice the warriors of WWII made for us. We both got choked up. It was something I should have said to him a long time ago. Thanks to Private Ryan for bringing this out in me.

That was my dad

My dad was one of those brave men who hit the beach before any of the other soldiers landed. The movie made me cry and gave me some understanding of why he won't talk about it. He and my uncle will only say that it was war and what they did was done for my freedom. I love and honor them for that.

I spoke to someone who saw the movie and his reaction disappointed me because he didn't get what those brave men did for us. Part of me is grateful that he doesn't have knowledge, but a greater part of me says that everyone should know how horrible it was. We only create more horrible ways to kill each other, and we need to be shown just how bad it was.

I am forever grateful to those men who fought for our country, and I am most grateful to have had every single one in my family return home.

I could hear my grandfather's voice

Two weeks ago, I lost my 73-year-old grandfather to cancer. He was a veteran of D-Day, participating in the first wave of the assault on Utah Beach and serving his unit as a medic at the age of 19. Until the very last months of his life, he never spoke about his wartime experiences.

When he finally did speak, the stories he told of hearing German voices only a few feet away behind the hedgerows, capturing and releasing three German nurses, physically knocking wounded men to the ground who were so full of adrenaline they didn't realize they were hurt, were absolutely shocking.

As I sat in my seat at the theatre, it was as if I could hear my grandfather's voice speaking to me, telling me to pay attention, that this was what he had experienced but could never reveal. After seeing "Saving Private Ryan," I have a better understanding of my grandpa and his life — and I'm very proud.

Here I am, Grandpa

My grandfather was one of the infantry on D-Day. I won't cheapen his experience by even pretending to understand the pain and suffering he went through in the war, and all the rest of his life remembering. He would always tell the seemingly "happy" stories of the war: how he was known throughout all the small French towns he passed through as the soldier with plenty of bubble gum for the children, and how he played golf on his few off-hours, but never a full eighteen because some of the holes were mined. I can't even remember how many times Grandpa told me how sandals were issued to the soldiers who wanted to protect their feet from the rock beach at Nice. His stories were as plentiful as bubble gum and just as prized by this lonely, French-speaking little girl.

My grandfather was not an important man in the scheme of things, the world did not change significantly because of his each and every action, but he was a good man who worked hard for every penny he earned and for the life he lived. After the war (he went as far as Berlin), Grandpa came home, had a family, made a living, lifted weights, and went ballroom dancing in his spare time.

This year I had a history seminar to research about World War I and World War II, and as I sat in church one Sunday, I made plans to call and interview him on these subjects when I got home. Grandpa died while I was in church. The terror, blood, and killing were never made known to me. That was the one story he never told.

So here I am, Grandpa, the same little girl who listened so eagerly to your tales; I'm ready to hear one more. Hello, Grandpa, are you there? Tell me.

Part Three

"Closure"

Overleaf photo: Sergeant John E. Sullivan. Courtesy of
Mr. and Mrs. Vincent F. Sullivan.

A closure for Mom

On June 12, 1944, my mother received the following telegram: *Harold killed in action, Mom not so good. Come home.*

My mother showed me the telegram after we had just seen the movie. We had talked about whether seeing the movie was a good idea for her. She's 80 and in failing health. Her family never got many details on the exact circumstances of his death.

She cried, I cried, for the entire movie and much of the evening after. She said she had never seen the invasion so realistically. Never have I been so moved by a movie. Never have I heard the stories Mom told about the war. Never do I want to have to live them. Thanks Dad, Uncle Harold, for serving. I never understood.

101st Airborne Division

My great-uncle jumped into Normandy with the 101st. Unfortunately, on the jump, he broke his leg. A French family took him in and hid him from the Germans until the Allies could rescue him. How lucky he was!

Two years ago, I visited the D-Day beaches at Normandy, where I gathered a small sample of the very sand my uncle and the other Allied forces jumped onto in June 1944. (Yes, it was a little bit illegal, but it was important sand!) I gave the sand to him and he was so moved by the gesture you would have thought that I gave him a key to the world! It did my heart good to know that I was able to give a little something back to him, even if it was only grains of sand.

My uncle died shortly after that, and his sons have now divided up the sand and each of them has a small piece of their dad's history.

Saving Private Ryan

For the first time in my life I realize that my own father is a hero.

Thank you, Granddaddy

Wow, my granddad really confused me when I followed his footsteps into the Marine Corps. He would talk about how proud he was to have served in the Corps during WWII, but he never talked about the bad. When I told him I had joined, I expected him to be proud I followed him. He instead asked why in the world would I do something like that. I questioned his "fun" stories about serving, and he said he just couldn't talk about the bad. He was proud when I graduated boot camp, and was proud when I fulfilled my commitment and came home. Thank you, God, for not putting us through what our senior citizens went through. Thank you, Granddaddy. Thank you, fallen soldiers.

Back to the future

My wife and I just viewed the movie here in Indianapolis yesterday. Awesome!! I have never exited a movie theater in my 70 years of viewing movies where you walked in silence, holding back personal tears as you remember the past. All I could think of was, what price democracy and freedom have required.

I told my grandson that he should see the movie (he's 16) to review the historical value that veterans in any war give to the meaning of freedom. I relayed that I was about 15 on June 6, 1944, sitting at a Chicago White Sox baseball game with my father, my twin brother, and my grandmother when they announced over the loudspeaker that Americans were landing on Omaha Beach. I didn't realize the personal closeness of this announcement until we received the news that one of my two cousins was killed before he ever got to the beach and that the other was on the beach trying to save lives. My cousin the medic never talked much about the invasion except that he carried a bag filled with safety pins which were used to suture up wounds, quickly. I never forgot that.

Cowardice

I was painting the house last weekend with my 26-year-old son when he said he wanted to see "Private Ryan." I had seen it the week before. "I'll see it with you if you want," I said. There was a four o'clock show; we could just make it. We put down our paintbrushes.

My father was a World War Two veteran: Burma, India theater. He arrived in Okinawa in August 1945, where he awaited the invasion of Japan that never happened. He was 36-years-old at the time.

I was 19 in 1969. A year earlier, I was ready to enlist. By the time of the draft lottery I was firmly against the war in Vietnam, but lucky enough (No. 254) not to have to decide how much I was against the war. I would have taken jail over Canada, but I never had to make the choice.

Vietnam has always haunted me. Not so much that I didn't go, but that we never understood what we had asked of the men and women who did go. Go fight a war we don't want to win. Go die for a cause nobody believes in. Then come home so we can spit on you, or worse, ignore you.

My son and I have always talked about war. The one both his Pop-pops fought in, and the one I did not. When he was a teenager I took him to see "Platoon," and we came out of the theater the same way — exhausted, speechless. He took his best friend to see the movie a couple of days later. Afterward I asked him about his friend's reaction to the movie that had moved us so much. My son replied, "He thought it was a war movie."

As we walked in silence out of the theater into the sun after "Private Ryan," my son finally spoke. "I almost had to walk out," he said. "It really bothered me."

The scene that upset him was the scene where the corporal sits weeping on the stairs as his friend screams in a room above while fighting for his life. It was excruciating. The hand-to-hand combat.

The final realization that the tables had turned. The sudden shout, "No! Wait, wait. Stop!" The whispered German as the knife was plunged deeper, deeper, deeper. And then the look on the face of the enemy and the coward as they passed each other on the stairs.

"That's every man's nightmare," said my son. "To be a coward like that. How could he live with himself after knowing what he did."

And I had thought that the height of bravery/cowardice was revealed on Omaha Beach. I believe my son understood the movie better. Sometimes surviving a war is the worst punishment for some who can never forget.

From a military wife

I saw the movie "Saving Private Ryan" with my husband, who is a United States Marine. It made me see the possibilities of what could happen to the most important person in my life. My father is also in the military, and therefore, I could lose the two most important men in my life.

Whether or not people liked the movie, it was real . . . and you need to take the time out to think about all of those soldiers who risked their lives, leaving behind the people they loved to give you freedom — you, people he doesn't even know. I am proud that my husband is in the military, willing to leave me behind to go and fight for your freedom. . . .

To all U.S. vets, I salute you

My father served in Vietnam. That is the only fact I know. He will not share anything of that part of his life with his family, and even as his son, I cannot demand that he do. To this day, you cannot touch my father to wake him if he is asleep. He will revert to those days lived moment to moment in the throes of war, where a second's lapse of attention could cost you your life.

I have seen, even in my own generation, the misinformed masses protesting any American involvement on foreign soil. I have heard the stories how Vietnam vets were welcomed home by yelling and screaming protesters, telling them to go kill some more. I cannot understand this.

To all U.S. Armed Forces Veterans, I salute you. I appreciate your effort, your sacrifice, and your love for the United States of America. On my next birthday, as I raise a glass to toast the coming of another year in my life, I will raise another glass to toast those who served, and most of all to my father, who is one of the greatest men I have ever known.

Lest we forget . . .

From the first 5 minutes of "Saving Private Ryan," I was crying. My dad was in WWII and participated in the beach landings. I remember him discussing the hedgerow infested with Germans, and the loss of many of his buddies, but there were many things he did not discuss with us. Every year my dad would march in the parade for Veterans of Foreign Wars and take very seriously the laying of the wreath and memorial service to our fallen soldiers. I lived through Vietnam and many of my high school classmates went off to war never to return, but not until seeing this movie did the whole picture come together and hit home. I am ashamed to say that even at my age, I am guilty of taking our freedom for granted and for thinking of war as something in the John Wayne movies.

Our country's attendance at parades honoring our veterans and those that have given their lives for their country has dwindled tremendously. Instead, Memorial Day in the United States means a day off from work and barbecues. Many people live with the residual pain of war all their lives and we are not even appreciative of what they sacrificed for us to live in freedom and we don't give them the credit they are due.

God forgive me for not being thankful for the men and women who gave to serve our country. Forgive our country for sweeping them under the rug. Please, through this movie, heal the wounds that are in the hearts of those that returned.

WWII vet with dementia still does not forget

I am a speech-language pathologist. Recently I was asked to help an 84-year-old nursing-home gentleman to create a "memory book" so that he could become oriented to the year, month, and place he is living. In his medical chart it stated "active combat WWII for 3 years as a Marine."

He is conversant, but forgetful of short-term memory. Long-term memory is intact, and I have been privileged since seeing the film to hear some of his stories. I have thanked him repeatedly for his service to us. Tears come to his eyes when I speak of it.

Some memories even Alzheimer's cannot erase.

A harsh reality???

The reality of the violence in this movie is never ending; there is never a time when the violence doesn't exist. There were scenes in this movie that only a veteran who has been in the field for more days than he can remember would understand. At night when you sleep, those who died don't go away — they stay with you. The smell of their bodies, the smell of the burning metal and equipment, the stupid conversations that take place is all about how war really was. . . .

Oh, say can you see . . .

I just got home from viewing "Saving Private Ryan" and I'm still shaking. Before seeing this movie, I was unfamiliar with WWII. Yes, I learned about it in school, but we were never told the graphic horrors of war. To prepare for this movie, my father and I rented "Patton" and "The Longest Day." Both are really good movies, but I don't think anything can prepare you for the carnage that was shown in that movie.

Both movies gave an overview of the events of WWII, but I was unprepared for the bloody slaughter that took place on Normandy Beach. I now have a strong and unrelenting pride in our flag. Each cross on Normandy is a single stitch in the American flag.

Think your life's tuff . . . think again

The next time you're laying in bed thinking about how much you hate getting out of bed to go to work, or school, or wherever you have to go . . . think about the men who had to go to work on that cold, rainy, miserable day. Think about the horrors they witnessed, the injuries they suffered, the pain they endured both physical and emotional. Think of the men who came home crippled and maimed for life, of the men who came home in boxes, and of the men who never came home at all. Think of the families reading the telegrams from the War Department that began, "We regret to inform you," and the families who would never hear anything at all.

Makes the daily grind seem a little less horrible. Doesn't it?

Every family around the world should see this film. Not because of the actors, or the story line, or the special effects that make it look so real. It was real. The millions of graves around the world can attest to that. Beneath those white crosses on the cliffs at Normandy and in Arlington National Cemetery, and in thousands of other cemeteries around the world, are the fathers, and the sons, and the brothers, and the uncles of families just like yours and mine. Every family around the world should see this movie so that we never forget the pain, the suffering, and the absolute horror that is war. Because every time someone forgets, another generation of young men dies and another field of white crosses is born.

Aug 14-44

Dear Sis

Please don't scold your little brother for not writing you sooner. He is very sorry. No killing Sis, I am almost ashamed to be writing now. When it has been so long ago. But you will make me very unhappy if you don't answere soon.

Well Well Well congratulation on the new arrival to your happy little family of yours. Another little girl yes huh. You know that is what I'm looking forward to somedays. To get married and have a home of my own. And sometimes I really get thinking about it, and it actually scares me. But I imagine that will be a long long time yet. silly arent I.

Well how are felling, I hope you are will and all. And Jerry how is he. He must of ~~it~~ had a terrible strain, I can just see Jerry now ~~paceing~~ pacing back and forth. Ah yes it must be wonderfull to be a poppa. I think I will be going for now but I will ~~wrote~~ write again soon

Love Bob

P.S. Gause the writing and how about a few pictures. Huh.

Robert Paul Fitzharris S¹⁄c
+ Div.

Poem for my uncle

A powerful symbol in the movie for me was the letters of the dying soldiers. It was clear that there must have been an unspoken rule among the soldiers which moved them to preserve the last letter written by the soldier after his death. Private Caparzo in his last breath asks Medic Wade to save his letter from the inevitable bloodstains. We later see Wade rewriting the letter to spare Caparzo's father the realities of his son's death. At the end of the movie, Pvt. Reiben dutifully takes out Captain Miller's last letter and places it carefully in his pocket. The letters remind me of the many letters my grandmother preserved from her brother during WWII. After my grandmother's death, my father shared his discovery of my uncle's last letter. For my grandmother at home they were the only connection to the war. I was only able to know my great uncle through her stories and his letters. After seeing the movie, I was able to understand him as a soldier. I wondered if one of his friends dutifully took his last letter to make sure it got home. I gained even more insight into the realities of his war and how he tried to protect his family from these realities. The movie and his last letter were the inspiration for the following poem:

Faded Words
Yellow pages,
Bring me back 56 years
to War experiences
I do not understand.

Memories limited by stories
Knowing the brother and Uncle,
but never really the soldier.

Faded Words,
Yellow pages,
A bond of a family
Strengthened for a
Moment in time by
a Soldier's last letter.

Photo left: Robert Paul Fitzharris, Seaman First Class, USS Houston. MIA, October 16, 1944. Courtesy of Mary Fitzharris Ogints. Letter courtesy of the estate of Helen Fitzharris Schmitz.

Through the perilous fight...

It didn't take this movie for me to shed tears. . . . I do whenever I visit Arlington or hear the sound of "Taps." You see, any man or woman who ever wore an American uniform, no matter what year or what war, is my SISTER or BROTHER!

From a retired USAF Senior NCO...

My father fought bravely offshore during World War II and the Korean War. I recently went to see "Saving Private Ryan" alone, as my dad passed away 6 years ago. I often asked my dad about the war. He was unable to talk about it most of the time, but there were brief moments when he would speak of the camaraderie between men and the fights, but even after the silly arguments they would still come together.

This movie showed me not only the brotherhood formed, but it also showed me the horrors that have gone unspoken.

Crying for mother...

I know this film was truly a "man's" film regarding fighting, brotherhood, bonding, etc., but as a young mother of two, my thoughts kept coming back to "what if they were my sons."

For my uncle

Although there were no black soldiers in "Saving Private Ryan," they were on Normandy Beach that day. My uncle was one of them. I never saw him sober in the 20 years I knew him. He went to work every day as a security guard and then left work and went straight to the bar. He never talked about the war. We used to laugh at him and ask why he got so drunk. He said that he couldn't sleep sober. Now I know why.

Saving Private Ryan

"Saving Private Ryan" was the best movie that I ever saw and I never want to see it again.

Part Four

"The Price of Freedom"

Overleaf photo: Staff Sergeant Vincent E. DeFelice, U.S. Army, 75th Division,
Belgium, circa 1944. Courtesy of Vincent E. DeFelice.

The price of freedom

There are a few people out there who just don't get it. Many are saying "Saving Private Ryan" was too violent and bloody. What do you people think war is? There is finally a movie that shows what our fathers and grandfathers had to go through so that we could sit here in the comfort of our homes and type on these damn computers. Freedom comes at a price. It is not, nor has it ever been, free!

I am told that I belong to "Generation X," that my generation could never understand. Well, when I was 19 years old, I was a U.S. Marine in the first group of men to cut through the Iraqi minefields, and I saw and experienced war. It was horrible. My friends died and I had to do things to other human beings that most other people only have nightmares about. The movie scared me and made me think about things that I have tried to suppress, but it also calmed some inner demons as well.

What I went through was bad, but it was over in a few short months, not like the four years that the men of WWII went through. Everyone in this country should find a WWII veteran or a person who lost a family member there, and thank them. None of us truly realize how fortunate we really are.

A remarkable piece of filmmaking

I saw "Saving Private Ryan" last evening and was numb afterward. Imagine your friends in high school and college that you meet frequently at the local pizza parlor, 17, 18, 19 years of age. . . . Instead, now they are in the LSTs approaching Omaha Beach with Germans firing machine guns at them. What incredibly brave young men who fought for this country and saved Europe and us from the Nazis.

Unfortunately, similar scenes (on land) occur today in Kosovo and on the Albanian border with Serbia. . . . Sure makes one hope for some rational thought and diplomacy. A far better way to solve conflict. . . . We don't need more 18 and 19 year old soldiers dying . . . nor do we need ethnic cleansing. . . .

History finally understood

During my junior high and high school years (and even after a course in college), I found studying history to be boring and irrelevant. Therefore, I never paid attention. I have always been under the impression that war was senseless and that there was no need to bring our American soldiers into the dealings of other countries.

Then a friend took me to see "Saving Private Ryan." I had no idea what kind of movie I was sitting down to. From the beginning of the movie, I was on the edge of my seat. I had to continually ask questions about what was going on and why, but I understand now. I've been looking into a lot of research on WWII and Vietnam because I now want to know all I can about why so many Americans died to help other countries.

From this day forth, I will never look at learning history in the same respect. Instead of closing my eyes and ears, I'll listen. . . .

Marine Huey Door-Gunner

Already three years in the Corps before I went to 'Nam in '68. But I was still green. It wears off fast, though, in combat. I remember how anxious I was to get assigned to a Huey helicopter gunship and get into combat so that I could earn my "Combat Air Crew" wings as a door-gunner. You were required to fly a minimum of twenty missions and be shot at by the enemy during three of them. I earned my wings during my first week! The tracers at night looked like the size of beers cans whizzing at you. The sound of hits on my helicopter scared the hell out of me. But nothing gripped me more than the sound of my friends when they took hits.

Mortar attacks freaked out everybody. You generally don't hear them coming. They just start blowing up around you. Then it's the same thing, more friends taking hits.

"Saving Private Ryan" was very moving in the way that the agony and total chaos of combat was depicted. It only lacked the smell, the touch, and the emotional reality of having been there.

Oh yes, I was quite proud to earn those "wings." They gave me recognition. But then I realized that there were 55 more weeks to repeat the first one.

When I rotated back to the U.S. a year later, I remember standing in the main hallway of San Francisco International while waiting for my flight home. Three girls walked up to two fellow Marines and myself and said, "Why don't you pigs go back to Vietnam and murder more people?"

Then one of the girls spit on my friend's shoe.

I told my friend, "Welcome home, Marine."

I am proud of you

You said, "I have so much respect for veterans from the past wars, I only wish I could tell them all and hug them and thank them." Young lady, you just did. As a Vietnam vet, thank you for your thoughts, and believe me, your hugs felt good.

Political context

It's interesting to me that so many people praise the selflessness of men risking their lives for Ryan, but so few of us are willing to be even moderately charitable in our modern lives. For everyone who thinks of this movie as a call to "earn it," please get motivated to give a few hours a week or a small portion of your income to the people around you who need saving. Between welfare reform and downsizing, whatever you think of those things politically, there are a lot of poor people near you who could use your help. Please be a hero in your own backyard.

Crosses

While stationed in Germany, my family had the opportunity to visit France. While there we visited Verdun, burial grounds for thousands upon thousands of American soldiers who died during WWI and WWII. It was overwhelming to see acres and acres of white crosses and realize how many men had died overseas in the name of freedom. Also in Verdun, a building stands, and in this building are bones and skulls. Many of these bones have never been identified. Many graves for loved ones stand empty due to the harsh reality of war.

I realized while watching "Saving Private Ryan" that although we can grasp a partial feeling of what it may have been like for the soldiers at Omaha Beach, and in every battle, we can never realize the full story, unless we were there ourselves to experience it. Thirty minutes of a film (the beach scene) cannot be enough time to make the audience fully grasp the situation. Expand your minds, people — this was not a film for entertainment, it was a film to try to make the young and old realize the harsh reality of war. War is not pretty, it is not glorious. If a dozen young people are changed by this film and made to realize that their lives and others are worth cherishing, so be it. We can only hope.

God Bless Every Man, Woman, and Child who has fought, died, or been victim of war.

We owe more than we can ever repay

I'm sitting here stunned, fighting back the tears. I've been in the Air Force for six years, and never once gave a thought as to what would happen if the U.S. became involved in a large-scale war again. Images from the movie are all too easily replaced with the faces of my friends and co-workers, who, I'm sure, are just as shocked as me. I also now realize that we in the U.S. give lip service to honoring vets for their achievements in the past but no one can ever repay the men who went through that hell for us. To watch your friends be killed in front of you, and continue to fight, is something I can't even fathom. My fear now is that if and when it's my turn, I won't be as brave as those who came before me.

Response to: We owe more than we can ever repay

We all have to pay our dues. Those guys in WWII were paying theirs to the ones who came before them and they to the ones before them all the way back to Valley Forge, Lexington/Concord, and Bunker Hill — and not just to the ones who served in combat, but to everyone who tries to make the world just a little better than it was. Those guys had some heavy dues to pay, but that was the breaks. They do deserve our respect for that, but so do you. It's no mark against you that there is no war for you to suffer in or that others are not in the service, either. Just do good. You don't have to get shot at to be "earning it."

Scary stuff

The movie was frightening but so is the reality behind it. Modern war is industrialized slaughter. The folks who fight wars aren't superhuman action figures with nerves of steel; they're folks like you.

The movie illustrated just how dangerous a battlefield is. I think it was the sounds of whizzing bullets, popping ricochets, and flying stuff that made the point. But consider this — the movie showed a war that ended 50 years ago. Imagine what's waiting on the battlefield now! I saw some footage of the Gulf War, and it was frightening to see just how "improved" the weapons were over what we had in the early 70s.

Yes, scary. In these days of superhero movies and action figures, we need to be pulled back to reality. This movie did just that.

It affected me in a way I could never imagine

I have never had a movie affect me as much as this one has. For the first time I find myself cringing from gunshots in a television show and switching channels if any "war" scene is being shown. After the movie was over, and the credits began to run, I felt as if I were drained, unable to comprehend the enormous sacrifice these men gave to their country. They not only gave their lives but their childhood, their innocence, and in some cases their humanity. We in this day and age of high tech missiles, smart bombs, and biological weapons have no concept of war as it was, and might be again. For those who think war will solve our problems, watch this movie and picture YOUR sons in the first 30 minutes.

What are the messages?

Do the means justify the end?
Does the end justify the means?
In "Schindler's List," one helped many.
In "Saving Private Ryan," many helped one.
Perhaps Spielberg wants us to look within ourselves and find how
we all can live with each other and all become a part of those who
follow us, whether in 5 years or 50 years or 500 years. . . .

Remember them all

Normandy. D-Day, the 6th of June, 1944. This event rightfully
elicits awe and respect for the sacrifices of the U.S., British,
and Canadian troops involved in this terrible and epic battle. I
cannot thank them enough.

But I am beginning to develop a concern triggered by the
postings to this message board that people will remain convinced
that D-Day was the battle that ended the war with victory for the
Allies and that the sacrifices of the American GIs were the greatest.
Our sacrifices are without question undeniable. But we Americans
repeatedly forget that we were only a part — albeit critical from a
material standpoint — of a larger Allied coalition, the majority of
whose members had been fighting for their lives against Nazi
tyranny for nearly three years prior to Pearl Harbor.

Do not mistake me. I am denigrating neither "Saving Private
Ryan" — a magnificent piece of filmmaking — nor the sacrifices,
both individual and collective, made by American servicemen and
their families during WWII. I count such veterans amongst friends
and family. I am merely seeking to remind my fellow Americans that
we owe a huge debt of gratitude to the (literally) millions of Russians
who died in the savage fighting on the Eastern Front.

The Eastern Front was the focal point of the war for Nazi

Germany, the ultimate focus of the Nazi dogma of race hate as exemplified by the Death Camps, the Einsatztruppen, the commitment of the major portion of Nazi Germany's armed forces to the Eastern front from 1941 until the war's end. More than 20 million Russians died from 1941–1945. Many were killed by their own paranoid security forces on the merest suspicion of dissent. The vast majority were killed either in battle or, in the case of Russian civilians in occupied territories, by the officially directed policies of "war without mercy" practiced by the German Armed Forces on the Eastern Front.

It was the Battle for Moscow in 1941 that stopped the German advance. Stalingrad marked the destruction of the huge German 6th Army. Kursk marked the total loss of strategic initiative on the eastern Front to the Russians, as well as the irreplaceable loss of vast amounts of material and experienced personnel. Battles of these sizes were never seen on the other fronts. The level of mutual savagery found on the Russian Front was often unparalleled elsewhere in WWII.

Whenever I remember the sacrifices of WWII veterans, of all they endured on our behalf, I always think of ALL veterans of the allied cause. It is to them that we owe a debt of eternal gratitude. Their sacrifices around the world saved all of us from the ultimate Dark Age of human history. I can never thank them enough.

Words cannot describe . . .

I am a 28-year-old male, and have seen this movie twice so far. No movie has EVER come close to touching me like this one. I have never been "into" war movies or history, but this movie changed something inside me. Like many of the posts that I have read, this movie opened my eyes. I used to make fun of, or have no patience for, some of the older folks I've been around, but now I understand where they come from, and what they have been through. Those vets have 100 times more guts than me. I now have some new heroes in my life.

Joe next door

The one thing that has always haunted me is that in real life as in the film, the men were "Joe next door." A teacher, a country boy, a writer, a lingerie salesman, a farmer. Ordinary men doing extraordinary things.

As a middle-aged male, I remember sitting in church on Sunday, and as the men went to the communion rail, I would ask myself, "What did he do in the war? He fixes my dad's machinery now, but where was he then? Was he a hero?"

I'm sure he was, as were they all.

Guilty! Guilty!

Have any of you experienced the feeling of complete guilt while watching ANY war movie?

I have a pain that hurts so deep that I cannot watch "realistic" (as defined by the critics) war movies. Most of them harbor too much Hollywood, lacking reality and substance. But this Spielberg movie approached too emotionally the feelings of combat: total chaos, fear to the nth degree, loud noise, crying without control, and the greatest impact — the feeling of guilt for having survived whereas others did not.

In the 1960s, I was stationed at Fort Bragg, NC. Among other duties, I was a death notification officer. At 6:30 in the morning I had to tell a mother, wife, or whomever that a son/husband was dead. I was also a survivor assistance officer, helping the family to plan the burial. That duty haunts me more than anything else I have done in the military.

After 32 years, I still cannot shake this tremendous feeling of guilt. I keep asking myself, "Why didn't I die there? What difference have I made for society because I lived?" I am retired now, after serving in public education all these years. I just hope and pray these young ones that I have been educating for so many years never have to experience the hell that our country will purposefully place upon them. And, even if they survive, will they feel that having cheated death, the result is a guilt complex so strong that it is a fulltime job trying to keep these emotions submerged?

I have to avoid situations where the flashbacks of emotions become too strong to experience. I attended sessions at the Vet Center, and they say that recalling helps overcome the emotions, but it just reminds me of that which I wish to forget. . . .

Women in combat? See this movie. . . .

It is my hope as a father and a veteran that all those politician clowns who are in such a rush to send my daughters into the hell of combat are forced to sit and watch this film. It is bad enough that wars are fought and good men die. Why are they in such a hurry to get our daughters into this hell?

Would our present liberal Commander-in-Chief send his daughter off into the hell of combat? I do not think so. She would be shipped off to a college overseas — to protest, I bet.

Sadly, today's political leaders merely look at the Armed Forces as a social club that occasionally goes off somewhere to beat up on some pissant country's pathetic excuse for a military. The military is not a college scholarship foundation nor is it a social laboratory. It seems to me that most politicians, and maybe even the citizens, have forgotten that it is our job to defend our nation's interests by killing people and blowing things up.

I have been fortunate in my service that the toughest conflicts I have been involved in were Desert Storm and Bosnia. My father fought in Vietnam (and was heckled and spat upon when he returned to the U.S.) and my grandfathers fought in World War II. I simply cannot fathom why the general consensus of the country seems to be that it is a good thing to send women into this hell — it is horrible enough for men.

Some people out there will call me chauvinistic, or worse. I do not care. Hopefully something larger and more important than Academy Awards will come out of this film. We need to seriously rethink our current policies — maybe this movie will start some of that process.

X generation vs. ???

The next time your "heroes" sing in concert or do a dance in the end zone, maybe you might want to re-evaluate the meaning of the word? And you just may realize the meaning of Memorial Day and Veterans Day! The sacrifices in real war are REAL . . . you can't just turn your little computer off and restart the program. . . .

I couldn't speak

This movie brought me to the closest I have ever come to understanding the sacrifices other men have made to make this world a better place. I'm 46 years old, but I feel like I've grown up some by watching this movie. If someone can die so bravely for the cause of mankind, why can't I live as bravely? Why shouldn't I live as bravely? If I had tried to speak at the end of this movie, I would have wept openly.

It wasn't the movie that moved me, it was the saga of all the suffering and death from all our wars that I never really appreciated. It awakened me to the fact that people I see in the grocery store have experienced these things. May God help us all to live the best life we can.

Why is this film important?

It's obvious, given the testimonials posted here, that many of us had little idea how brutal war is, and consequently we have had a thin appreciation of the bravery and sacrifice of those who have served their country. Stories like the Normandy invasion must be told, but they also must be understood. By bluntly depicting the carnage of D-Day, Spielberg tells the story with a clarity and resonance that most Americans have never known, and in doing so he honors these men.

Do not dismiss this enlightenment as insubstantial because it's inspired by cinema. The motion picture arts as a whole do not deserve the reputation that Hollywood has established. Great films have always, and will always, be produced, even as many Hollywood pictures continue to degrade humanity and insult our intelligence. Words do not reign supreme as a form of expression. We need pictures and music as well. (For centuries, Michelangelo's painting of "The Final Judgment" has impressed millions of viewers with the weight of words written by St. Paul.)

As a work of art, "Saving Private Ryan" may succeed as one of this century's most eloquent statements on the subject of war and its miseries. I think it is evident that the great majority of those who watched the film have gained a greater understanding of why we must honor our veterans, why we must honor the memory of the fallen, and why we must honor the debt that we owe them. Keep reading and listening to what people are saying. There already appears to be a transformation of consciousness happening on a mass scale, across generational lines. This is what cinema is meant to do.

The first realistic portrayal of war shown in a movie

"Saving Private Ryan" made me realize what war is really all about. This may sound immature and naive, but before seeing this movie I always pictured war as being an honorable and courageous way to defend your country. After the first ten minutes of the film, I quickly realized the true nature of war. I saw these young men scrambling to survive and not being concerned about being a hero. Just not being paralyzed with fear took a great amount of courage.

Another thing this film brought to my attention was that the captains and generals didn't win the war. It was the unknown privates and lieutenants who saved the world from a dark fate. It's sad how long it took us to honor these young courageous war veterans. Now, as we finally see a true portrayal of war, it shows us how no human being should ever have to be exposed to such an unspeakable hell. . . .

16-year-old guy

When the movie ended, no one got out of his or her seat. We all watched as the American flag just waved in the air. Five minutes later, everybody was still in their seat, quiet, except for those with no conscience, who left early. One person had the nerve to clap — that person was me. After that the crowd erupted, standing ovations all through the theater.

As we were going to the car, I asked my father, who did not serve in the war, what he thought. A man who always says, "It was okay, could have been better," said, "It was powerful, I have nothing to say." That's when I knew that he also knew this movie was a masterpiece. Forget about a movie with a boat sinking. How about a movie with hearts churning, people thinking, and understanding?

Reflection from an earlier war

On September 17, 1862, the battle of Antietam was fought in western Maryland. This single day is still the bloodiest in American history. Using the latest high-tech medium of that day, Matthew Brady sent photographers Alexander Gardner and James Gibson to the scene of the battle. With the cameras of those days, action scenes could not be shot; all of the images were of the aftermath, and of the dead.

Later, Brady opened an exhibit in his New York gallery titled "The Dead of Antietam." The following appeared in the "New York Times":

> *"The dead of the battlefield come up to us very rarely, even in dreams. We see the list in the morning paper at breakfast, but dismiss its recollection with the coffee. . . . Mr. Brady has done something to bring home to us the terrible reality and earnestness of war. If he has not brought bodies and laid them in our dooryards and along streets, he has done something very like it."*

I flew with the mighty 8th

During April, May, and the first few days of June, 1944, I had the opportunity to see, meet, and drink with some of the 17-, 18-year-old, or even "older guys" (maybe 20 years old). We were drinking British beer together in the town squares of Northampton, Kettering, and the likes of The Midlands of England. We were also fighting each other over who'd be the "bloke" who'd have the last dance before the bartender would say, "Time, Gentlemen," and no more would be served that night. And, "You Yanks better hurry or you'll miss the Liberty Trucks that will carry you back to your bases."

I flew with the Mighty 8th. Those "Yanks" would be on the beach or floating in the water of the beaches of Normandy. We could not drop the bombs from our B-17s because we did not know how far our troops had advanced. That was at 9:30 AM, June 6, 1944. We returned to our base with those bombs. At 1:30 PM we were back again; once again we could not help the guys, the 18-, 19-, and 20-year-olds who made the landings or died on the beaches, because we were afraid we would drop on our own troops. So, the bombs that might have helped them were returned to base in England.

Spielberg's film brought the memories of that day home to me and, I am certain, to many of the survivors of the landings and the missions flown by the 8th AF.

Too violent or too thoughtful?

How many people, I wonder, would object to the violence if "Ryan" were a film about Vietnam? How many of you took the trouble to voice your objections to the violent combat of "Platoon"?

I think the reason is that depictions of Vietnam violence allow us to sit smugly and say, "Oh yes, this is terrible, this is why I was so against the Vietnam War," or "We all know Vietnam was a big mistake, and this film just shows us how right we are."

The importance of "Ryan" is that it shoots those comfortable, self-satisfied notions right between the eyes. We are not in the habit (for excellent reasons) of saying that it was a big mistake to fight the Axis. Here is a taste of what American soldiers suffered, lived through, and died in, in service of a cause that no rational person would call wrong. And it doesn't sit too well on a stomach full of smug assumptions like "All violence is wrong" and "War is never the way to solve anything."

Maybe that revulsion you feel isn't in your stomach at all. Maybe it's your brain trying to turn over.

Part Five

"Thank You for My Life"

Overleaf photo: First Lieutenant David Leibowitz, U.S. Air Corps.
Reported missing in flight, India Burma theater, April 10, 1945.
Courtesy of Eva Zieger.

Thank you

To all the veterans out there, I just want to say "thank you" from all of us young, cocky American kids who take for granted every day the freedom that we have only because you and your friends and brothers put your lives on the line.

I have to admit that this movie really woke me up to the fact that people actually do get killed, and they cry for their mothers, and that war is horrible and scary. And I got these feelings from sitting in a padded chair in an air-conditioned movie theater with five of my best friends.

I can't even begin to fathom how it was to really be there. People who list a movie star or sports figure as their hero need to have their heads checked out. From what I saw, if the hype is true and that was really an example of the reality of war, all of you veterans should be the only heroes on this earth.

It's because of you that I can write this message, that I can freely express my opinion, that I can do as I please, be whatever I want, and lead my life the way I want. We all owe you our lives. Thank you to each of you brave men from the bottom of my heart.

It's just too bad that it took a movie to wake this country up, including myself. I know one thing's for sure — I will never experience Memorial Day the same way again. Thank you for my life.

We can't ever forget

I had no idea what war was really like until I saw "Saving Private Ryan." I know this movie wasn't even as bad as it really was, but I'm sure it comes close. At first I didn't really want to see this movie because I had heard how graphic it was, but after hearing the reviews I knew I had to see it. My mother told me I owed it to my grandfather who fought in WWII. I also owed it to everyone that has fought in war and to everyone who gave his or her life for my way of life.

I have to say it was one of the best movies I have ever seen. I walked out of the theater with a newfound respect for veterans and all they had to go through. It saddens me to think so many had to die for our freedom.

My grandfather was involved in WWII, but he never once spoke of it to me. I was his little granddaughter and I wasn't supposed to know the horrors he went through. I didn't ask him about it. I didn't really care. It didn't affect me, or at least I didn't think so.

I will never get the chance to ask him about it and thank him. He died two years ago from leukemia. It seems like such a loss now. I'm so afraid the horrors of war will be forgotten and it will happen again in my lifetime. I know it is up to me and my generation to make sure no one forgets. I hope to become a history teacher and I will do my best to show the next generation what war was really like. It will be hard since I have never really experienced war, but I will do all I can to tell the truth. I feel I owe it to every single veteran to tell what really happened, and maybe "Saving Private Ryan" will help me to do that. I hope so.

This movie enriched my spirit and brought me closer to mankind!

I have been ashamed most of my life that I did not participate in the Vietnam War, as so many of my friends, my brother, and thousands of others did. I still don't believe in such a "war." I was a conscientious objector who asked to participate in a non-combatant capacity, but I was never called up.

My brother came back entirely changed, and some of my friends didn't come back at all. I am mainly ashamed because I wish that I could know what my brother learned that changed his life, but which he is unwilling to discuss. I feel that I have become separated by my not going to war, and I miss the closeness we used to share.

Thank you Mr. Spielberg, Mr. Hanks, and all the others who made this movie one of the most profound experiences of my life. I am proud not only that I wept openly many times during the movie, but that my teenage son (a very tough acting kid) said, "Anyone who doesn't cry at this movie isn't normal." Now I feel that I have reached much closer than ever to my changed brother and others like him. The absolute chaos and desperate struggle for survival this movie depicted seems so much more realistic and true to the sacrifices of our families and other Americans for generations that it makes me more grateful and proud of them than ever before. Thank you all again!

A teenager's point of view

When I went to see "Saving Private Ryan," I went with the expectations of a typical Hollywood film version of war. You know: a clean death, no gore, and a regular John Wayne movie that I was always told about.

My mom and I went together and as soon as the movie started, tears sprang to my eyes. The first battle scene was so incredibly unbelievable. I now finally understood what my grandfather always talked about. The incredible sacrifice that those brave young soldiers made was and still is a great inspiration to all of us young teens. Throughout the entire movie, tears poured and poured down my face.

The realization that my grandfather's old war stories weren't "stories" totally shocked me. They were all true, and all became quite vivid for me. I just wanted to thank Steven Spielberg and everyone who made and contributed to this incredible movie. I couldn't have learned and experienced any of this in any history class.

Teens ARE ignorant —
a 16-year-old viewpoint

To all apathetic teenagers:

I've always known that most of you don't care about your history. Hell, I've been in class with you. When asked, I've watched half of you answer that December 7, the date which was supposed to live in infamy, is simply the day after St. Nick's. I've also been in class with you while watching grainy footage from D-Day, and I've listened to you laugh as soldiers (same age as you, I might add) crumple into the sea seconds after stepping off the landing craft.

I used to accept your indifference as part of the puerile teenage mindset, and hoped that after seeing "Saving Private Ryan" you might change your mind. I was wrong. As I was walking out of the theater, I overheard clusters of you telling your friends how you thought the plot was rather boring, but the explosions, guns and the heaps of blood were "like, totally awesome."

Shame on you.

You and I have never experienced (thank God) the fear and terror of having our safety threatened, but that is no excuse to laugh at these citizen soldiers who died slow, excruciating deaths to give the right of freedom to you.

Freedom is not free. Have you earned it?

A teen who's been moved . . .

Hello. I'm a 13-year-old girl, and my father took me to see "Saving Private Ryan." It is by far the most moving movie I have ever seen in my short life. I know that I'll probably never experience such a harrowing thing as war in my lifetime, what with such advances that have gone on, but "Ryan" truly gave me some insight into what such a huge conflict is like.

This movie gave me a window of sorts so that I could witness the ugliness of war. I'm very happy that this movie wasn't sugarcoated like so many other WWII movies I've seen. Many other war films have a dashing hero who saves everyone and gets out alive himself. But "Ryan" had real people who weren't trying to be heroes, just helping for the cause.

Of course I cried. I mean, who wouldn't? After seeing "Ryan," everything else seemed so . . . I don't know, extravagant, I guess you could say. This film has made me feel a sense of pride. Pride for the good men, the soldiers who put their lives on the line for freedom, for peace, for humanity. I thank anyone who has fought on the line.

What a friend and I learned

When my friend and I went to see "Saving Private Ryan," we expected to see another war film like all the others that we have seen. We are both teenagers and at one point had glorious visions of going into battle and defeating the evil Communist (or other) foe. After the first scene in this movie, our opinions on war were dramatically changed. The sheer horror and tragedy of war was captured in this one film.

How your companions, friends, and even family can be sentenced to death by one stray bullet. And you are helpless. The emotional and physical stress our grandfathers had to endure was amazing. This movie has forever changed my view on war and its brave veterans. I salute the survivors of not just WWII but also Vietnam, the Gulf War, etc. . . .

Humbled

I saw the movie last night and the feeling I came away with was humility. I've never felt so undeserving in my life. The idea that these veterans of WWII went freely and gave of themselves in such a manner brought a feeling of unworthiness. In the times we live in, we can only imagine how it must have been during that time.

I am very proud to be an American and have always been, but I never realized how much I've taken for granted living in a society of free citizens. There is no way to explain to these courageous men and women how honored I am for what they have done for me; furthermore, there is no way of thanking them. All I can say is that I will no longer take my freedoms for granted and that your sufferings have not gone by unnoticed. Thanks all of you from the deepest part of my being. I both honor and adore you veterans who have given this gift to me. Thank you for your bravery and God bless all of you.

From a younger generation . . .

This was one of the most moving movies I've ever seen. I am only 14 and this movie is a real wake-up call for my generation. I never dreamed war was like that but I never really thought about it either. Yeah, people my age always hear about how horrible it was and this and that and it's like "Blah blah blah." And I was like, "Just get over it, ok?"

But now I see what those people really went through and I couldn't imagine a more horrific experience. During the invasion in the movie, I was just sitting there with my jaw dropped. I can't even imagine how someone could go on after being in something like this. I NEVER dreamed it was like that. And I felt so sorry for Mrs. Ryan — just imagine losing all of your sons, everything you worked so hard for and loved so very much. So it was extremely important that they went and saved James Ryan.

I'm only 14 . . . but it hit me hard

I am only 14 years and I went to see "Saving Private Ryan" with my parents. I've been through ups and downs in my life and thought of dying often, but for those men who died, the second the plank came down . . . well, they'd give two seconds of my breath to go home to their families.

For those of you who thought the plot sucked and it was a horrible movie, wake up and smell the coffee. Half of it wasn't a plot. He lost his brothers and many more people died in the war — that's what happens. Face the fact that this is what war is like. . . .

Overwhelmed

It didn't hit me right away. A tear or two by the time credits rolled. Sitting there, mind a jumble of flash images. Stark sounds of combat still echoing in my ears. I hit the exit and was blinded by sunlight and I walked slowly to a nearby bench. The sky was beautiful and it was like seeing it for the first time. The air seemed pure and fresh. I had just come from a vicarious experience of history. Of war. Of hell. I kept telling myself, "This is the closest I want to come to being in combat. Every few minutes a grief would find anchor somewhere inside and I could feel it welling up, touching the eyes, trembling the chest. I made it home in a daze.

At home, among the familiar objects, among the silence of these walls, I sat down and wept. I didn't truly understand what I was weeping for. The loss. The carnage. The horrendous reality of what they went through. Guilt for having never been in a position to do something as meaningful as saving a life. Guilt for not honoring those who have fought and died for our country. No matter, the tears came and they unblocked something within me.

I will never look at another war film in the same way. I will never think of war in the same way. For a film to do this to me, regardless of any cinematic or narrative fault you may choose to bring up, is remarkable.

To all the veterans, men and women, to those who survived and to those who didn't, my heartfelt appreciation, respect, and undying thanks. And to Steven and crew, you have made a film for the ages.

My heart still aches!

I have never witnessed the casualties or brutality of war firsthand, but I had several cousins and an uncle die in WWII, and I shed many tears for them during this movie even though they died before I was born. I am still shaken and will never see combat the same way again.

From the time the movie started till it ended, the theater was completely silent. You could actually "feel" what everyone else was feeling — utter horror and sorrow for all the precious men and boys who lost their lives so that my family and I can safely live in America. Yes, this movie is about "Saving Private Ryan," but in another sense, isn't it about saving our freedom and preserving humanity?

I was so impressed by the direction of the actors in that Spielberg never let them lose their realism. There were never confrontations fueled by testosterone which seem to be par for the course for war movies, but rather a brotherhood. All the soldiers realized each other's weaknesses and accepted them. I thought that in itself was a breakthrough.

I also came away from this picture feeling as if I had been placed in the middle of a war. I hated war to begin with, but this movie made me have even more contempt for combat. I really believe if it were feasible, that if everyone on the face of the earth today could see this movie, there would be no more wars.

In closing, I would like to thank Mr. Spielberg and Tom Hanks for "Saving Private Ryan."

Only tears . . .

I cannot express how emotional I became concerning the first 5 minutes of this movie. When the old man bends downs at the gravesite and begins to cry; man, anyone who has ever lost a loved one and who has visited that place of final burial cannot help but cry. But to know these young men who never really had a chance to experience life because of having to fight a war on distant shores and losing their lives for freedom is so touching to anyone's soul.

God bless the soldiers who died, God bless the people who took time to make a movie like this, and God bless every soul who gave up an afternoon to go see this movie. By seeing this movie we finally may truly honor those men and women who died so long ago. Let us never, never forget that War is Hell but Freedom is heavenly.

And "only tears" can fully lay to rest those who gave all for the world.

Politicians should fight wars

I'm a paramedic in a big city. We often pick up veterans and they are mostly drug-addicted alcoholics who want to get rehab in the hospitals. They are really messed up. Well, I saw "Saving Private Ryan" and after that I had so much respect for veterans and what they did for our country.

The other day my partner and I got a call from a guy who wanted to go to the hospital. He said he was addicted to crack, marijuana, and alcohol and wanted help. This guy's hair was falling out, he was pale. I asked him if there was anything else wrong and in the midst of my sarcasm he said, "I'm a Vietnam vet, ex-Marine." Just then I realized it was not his fault his life was so messed up now; he was one of the guys who risked his life for our country. Just as I was about to leave him, I asked if he ever saw the movie "Full Metal Jacket." His response was: "No, I WAS Full Metal Jacket."

I thanked him, and told him he doesn't get the credit he deserves.

I had no idea

I'm 14 years old. I've always thought that I paid attention to what was going on around me and that I also paid attention to history. Until I saw "Saving Private Ryan," I thought that I mostly understood how horrible war is. I was wrong.

I know now when I look in the mirror that I'm lucky to be able to look in my own mirror, in my own house. . . . I don't dash under bullets in war zones. . . . I haven't held my friend in my arms, watching him die, hearing him calling for his mother as he gasped his last breath of air. I've never left my spouse . . . knowing that there was a good chance that I'd never see him again.

War is pure hell. That's what I've learned. I know that I will never fully be able to understand and take in everything that happened there, because I wasn't there. But, "Saving Private Ryan" was as close as I'll hopefully ever come to knowing the true horrors of war. I now know to not only live for the future . . . but to live for the past also . . . and that is so very important for me to understand, and I'm glad that I do.

Thank you 1,000 times over from an 18-year-old girl

Growing up in the early eighties and living life as a teenager in the nineties may tend to make one ungrateful and somewhat unaware of the freedom that Americans truly do possess. Until last night, I was one of those ungrateful Generation X-ers. After work, a group of friends and I made our way to the local theater to watch a movie that our parents had been raving about. In the car, we talked about our day, listened to loud music, and generally acted like typical teenagers. We were excited to see a movie about which we literally knew nothing; previews and movie promos have a tendency to do that.

We bought our tickets, made our way past the snack bar, and plunked ourselves down in our seats. The previews had just ended; we were right on time. The moment "Saving Private Ryan" started, the tears started to flow and they didn't stop until the ending credits rolled. The movie horrified me and gave me a wake-up call that was much needed. Who knew that war could be so devastating? I surely didn't. Schoolbooks give very little detail to the "battle parts" of war. Text reads something like this: "The day was bleak and many people died." What? That's it?

Reality paints a different picture, one that shows war as bloody, painful, and traumatizing to the people who went through it and the friends and families of those who fought. I pray that the future doesn't hold more pain and devastation like that expressed in the wars and battles fought thus far by our great nation. To all the veterans still gracing this earth with their presence, I say "thank you" from me and all future generations to come. You helped mold this country into what it is today: a haven for freedom. Without your courage and love for humanity, I might not have the freedom to type this letter to you and express my most sincere gratitude. God bless.

A sincere apology to all veterans

I apologize for never truly appreciating what you did for us. I was naive and foolish. I took for granted all of this freedom that you risked (and for some, gave) your life for. As the movie came to a close, I was speechless. The only word I managed to utter was "damn." I never knew the horrific ordeal that all of you went through. I cried for the first time while watching a movie. It was so tragic, so devastating.

"Earn it"

Dear Mr. Spielberg,

I was raised in an Army patriarchy. I went fishing with men of 20+ years of experience, E6's, E7's, E8's galore. These men served under my grandfather in two conflicts and a World War.

Throughout my childhood I yearned to be a man during my grandfather's time. I wanted to storm the dunes of Tunis with him and parachute into Sicily. I read every book I could find in the public library and asked for rare or more expensive new volumes for birthdays. By the age of 10, I could list and count the table of command and order of battle for most units involved in any action of the European theater, including Waffen SS and Wehrmacht.

The movie was technically perfect. Where did they get those Marders and Tiger tanks? How could they have made this film for only 60 million dollars?

"Saving Private Ryan" has opened up my deep secret place and shown me how it was and could have been for me, my grandfather, or for the sixty thousand on that beach. I'm not sure how I've been affected; I'm still feeling out the movie. What I do know is that my life is filled with all the blessings of that generation of Allies who had the chance and the courage and the moral fiber to fight the Allied fight.

My love for the common soldier will always remain true, but for now I have learned to consider those that died and those that lost them. More than ever, I am thankful that they sacrificed their lives for our country and for my grandfather.

"Saving Private Ryan" is as much a story about the horror of war to me as the rewards of war. Today we have the rewards of WWII: computers, faster cars, space travel, children like us. Our KIA surrendered more than their lives on those beaches; they surrendered their own futures and us. Captain Henry Miller's last breath, "Earn it," should apply to more than Private James Francis Ryan.

God knows that has affected me more than anything else in the movie, much less anything else to have come along in a very long time. Suddenly my career, home, and all things I hold dear appear undeserved, as I have not earned them. I did not die on Omaha or Utah Beach, neither did Private Ryan. I, too, will have to remember what has been sacrificed for me and to try harder and show to myself that there is more to life than being ahead and living through my own private battles.

Yes, I've become moody since seeing this film. Yes, I've called my family members, and yes, I've visited the local National Cemetery in the Presidio. When this survivor's guilt wears away, I'm sure I'll have lighter feelings, surprise, and delight at the movie. But until then, thank you for making this important film. I hope that others of my generation view this and learn a little respect for everything they have available to them today.

NOTE: *This AOL member wrote us to add that the effect of the film lasted for weeks. Then he spoke to an infantryman who'd fought on Omaha Beach. "It was my pleasure," said the veteran. With that, the AOL member felt relieved.*

The paradox

Did you notice that with the exception of the REMF who was chosen because he could speak French and German, almost all the characters in the critical scenes were the absolute most elite troops either side had to offer? Rangers . . . Pathfinders . . . 101st AB . . . 82nd AB . . . S.S. Panzer units. . . . The point is that the very best . . . the real "Rambos" . . . were just average Joes led by a schoolteacher.

From a retired USAF Senior NCO . . .

In the theater today, there were many veterans of WWII. My town in California is a 70% retired community, and many residents are WWII vets. Several had to get up and take breaks to go outside and cry. Many couples were softly sobbing throughout the movie, holding hands. One woman cradled her husband's head and kissed him in front of us all, saying "Hank, I thank God you came home alive!" I'm glad he came back too, and I am grateful for what he (and the others who didn't come back) did for the world. These, then, are the only valid critiques of the film, not the inane comments by the uninformed. The fadeout on the flag was much more symbolic for all of us than most will recognize.

I wanted to take this opportunity to share with you a ceremony that's very near and dear to my heart. It is a ceremony I was proud to narrate for many years during formal military dinners. It is known as the Fallen Comrade Salute, written by a retired army lieutenant colonel, and modified to include those Killed in Action as well as those Missing in Action and Prisoners of War. It is conducted in darkness, with a sole spotlight on the white-gloved hands of a ceremonial guardsman, who carries an empty helmet to the table at the start, and accompanies the narrator after first lighting a white candle on the table. This candle burns during the entire dinner, to honor our Fallen Comrades. The ceremony goes like this:

<dim house lights; guardsman enters the mess with helmet>

Ladies and gentlemen, before we rise to post the colors, there are members of our mess who are missing. Please be seated while we acknowledge them. . . .

As you entered the ballroom this evening, you may have noticed a small table here, in a place of honor, near our head table. It is a table set for one. Please, let me explain.

Military tradition is filled with symbolism, and this table is our way of symbolizing the fact that members of our Profession of Arms are missing from our midst. They are commonly called Prisoners of War, Missing in Action, and Killed in Action. We call them Fallen Comrades. They are unable to be with us this night, so we honor them in this way.

This table set for one is small, symbolizing the frailty of one prisoner, alone, against his oppressors. REMEMBER!

The tablecloth is white, symbolizing the purity of our Fallen Comrades' intentions to respond to their country's call to arms. REMEMBER!

The single rose displayed in the vase reminds us of the families and loved ones of our comrades in arms who keep the faith awaiting their return. REMEMBER!

The red ribbon tied so prominently on the vase is reminiscent of the red ribbons worn on the lapels and breasts of thousands who bear witness to their unyielding determination to demand a proper accounting of our missing. REMEMBER!

The slice of lemon is on the bread plate to remind us of their bitter fate. REMEMBER!

There is salt upon the bread plate, symbolic of the families' tears as they wait. REMEMBER!

The glass? The glass is inverted. They cannot drink with us this night. REMEMBER!

The chair? The chair is empty. They cannot be with us this night. REMEMBER!

Remember, all of you who served with them and called them comrade, who depended upon their might and aid and relied upon them, for surely, they have not forsaken you.

<TAPS is played on the bugle, spotlight on white gloves holding an empty helmet>

A quote from a stone in Normandy

There is a quote on a stone near the Allied cemeteries in Normandy. I may not get it exactly right, but the meaning is there. It states simply:

For your tomorrow, they gave their today

It says it all. Thank you to the veterans who served in all of our wars on all battlefields. We owe you more than we will ever fully realize.

Part Six

"A Great
Generation"

Overleaf photo: Dr. Stanley Fisher of New York, U.S. Navy,
Great Lakes Naval Training Station, Illinois, April 1945.
Courtesy of Dr. Fisher.

I now remember

When I was a kid, every November 11 (Canadian Remembrance Day) my mother would take my sister and me to Toronto, pin poppies to our coats, and watch the veterans lay flowers at the grave of the Unknown Soldier. We then observed one minute of silence at 11 AM. My mother felt that from a very young age we should understand that there was a price to pay for our freedom.

Now, living in the U.S., I (like everyone else I know) ignore these days of memorial and enjoy the holiday.

After seeing "Saving Private Ryan" I am ashamed that I have forgotten why I am able to enjoy my wonderful life. Make no mistake, next Remembrance Day and Memorial Day, I will take my children to pay tribute to those whom we will never be able to thank enough for their sacrifice.

Thank a veteran

I am going on 13 years in the Air Force and 35 years as a "tough guy." But I cried for the entire 30-minute Omaha Beach landing. Every young congressman who has never been near or associated with the military should see this movie. It just might make them think for a moment the next time they say veterans have it "too good" and constantly betray their country's promise to these men and women by hacking away at their retirement benefits and medical care.

We could give each one of these men $1,000 every day of their lives, and it wouldn't be enough. That goes for every war and every soldier. Who cares about who was in this movie and how hunky somebody looked? This movie was as close to real history as this generation will ever get.

Thank a veteran the next time you see one.

For all young soldiers, sailors, airmen, and grunts

Going to the PX/BX or commissary is a pain. All those old codgers, retired guys, and slow folks are always in your way. I usually get real pissed off because I'm in a hurry and have to slow down for them.

The other day I happened upon a couple of old guys in the Burger King. They were talking about their past battles. At first, I only listened with partial interest, then I became quite startled by their tale. The sheer bravery and devotion to duty these guys spoke of made me feel proud.

I gazed upon them with new and renewed respect. How awesome that these two frail old gentlemen suffered so much, so willingly, so I could regard them with such contempt in their golden years. You want to talk of VALUES and COURAGE, DEDICATION and DEVOTION to your country? Talk to the old guys and learn something.

GOD BLESS EACH AND EVERY ONE OF YOU OLD SOLDIERS AND SAILORS, AIRMEN AND MARINE GRUNTS! MY THANKS AND RESPECT ARE YOURS. I ONLY HOPE I CAN CARRY THE BANNER AS WELL AS YOU DID. You can rest assured I will from now on PATIENTLY wait for you. . . . It is the least I can do.

This movie

This movie should be shown along with "Born on the 4th of July" in Congress and the Senate before young men are sent to war.

My grandfather

As I sat watching this movie all I could think about was my grandfather. He passed away this last May at the age of 83. He rarely mentioned the war to me. When I was going to Europe my junior year of college, he spoke of being in the U.K., France, or Germany but not in any great detail. He landed on Omaha Beach in the second wave, which took 45% losses. After D-Day he marched across Europe to the Elbe where his division was the first to link up with the Russians at the Elbe River. Somehow he survived and returned to his small town on the east coast.

When he died this year we had an honor guard at his funeral. I can honestly say it was one of the most touching things I've ever witnessed.

I don't know what I'm trying to say really. I just want people to realize that men like my grandfather left their homes in small towns to fight for something that was intangible and something that we all take for granted. Freedom. Most of the GIs had never been out of their states, much less the country. They traveled across the ocean knowing they might never return. The Tom Hanks character is Every Man, exactly what the GIs were. These men were not John Wayne.

Time tends to make people forget. I'm 28, and I know people of my generation take everything for granted. They need to see this movie. They need to understand what these men sacrificed — that there was a time in our not-so-distant past when evil did exist in the world and these men rose up to fight back against it and in the process saved a large portion of the world.

I just want to say thanks to the men and women like my grandfather. We cannot comprehend the hell these people endured. "Saving Private Ryan" gives a glimpse of it. If you have a grandparent who served in WW2, give them a hug and say thanks for securing the world that you are fortunate enough to inherit.

I never cry at movies

But this was so different. I saw the film last night with my 73-year-old mother. My dad, who died 5 years ago at age 70, was a veteran of WWII. He was a medic in the Navy and saw brutal action in the South Pacific. My mother wept throughout the movie and watched the most violent scenes without flinching. I had to look away many times, especially during the first part. I just kept welling up with tears.

While I knew intellectually that Dad had suffered and witnessed many horrible things during the war, he chose almost never to discuss it with any of us. He just said, "Never look back." He'd receive invitations to reunions with his shipmates but never considered attending them. I think he was afraid that if he started to remember too much, he would break down. He was so determined to always be strong. I kept thinking how young he was when he endured all of that, just like those young men in the movie, and how brave they all were in spite of their youth.

I was left wondering whether Dad would have seen the film, if he were still alive now. I tend to think not, because it would have opened too many old wounds. Perhaps he might have though, in a sort of tribute to those friends who didn't make it back. I'll never know the answer.

I gasped in the first scene, when James Ryan was walking up to the cemetery as an elderly man. The clothes he was wearing, every detail, were precisely like my dad in his final years. He was the gentle grandfather to a bunch of little girls. Someday, when my daughter is older, I will want her to watch this movie, and appreciate the sacrifices her Granddad's generation made.

I was always grateful for having such a strong and loving Dad. My gratitude to him today, and to all of his generation, runs far deeper. I think their generation was so steady and reliable in raising and supporting their kids, in part because they felt they had a duty to be "good men," as the elderly Private Ryan said. You were all of that and more, Dad. I'm so proud to be your daughter.

Have we earned the sacrifice these men laid down for us?

Where did we get such men?

A great generation

As the years have passed, I have grown to love the women and men from the WWII era more and more. They suffered through the Great Depression and then were thrown into WWII. When I look at pictures of them, they all look so beautiful, so peaceful.

During the 50th anniversary of the end of WWII, I thank God I took the time to go to my uncle's house and thank him for what he had done for my country and me. He is a decorated, disabled veteran from WWII. He cried. My aunt said that was the first time she had ever seen him cry over the war.

After watching "Saving Private Ryan," I think we all ought to go out and hug the men and women from that era for the sacrifices they made for us. They are getting older. Don't miss your chance.

Following page: First Lieutenant David Leibowitz (second from right) and friends.
Photo courtesy of Eva Zieger.

Part Seven

*"Don't Worry,
Mom . . ."*

Jan. 28, 1942

Dearest Mother:

How are you, mom? I received your very nice letter & I was awfully glad to hear from you. I received all the letter of recommendation and my income tax check. Thank Dad for getting that stuff for me, I appreciate it very much. It is certainly swell to have a family like ours behind me, I know that I will always have someone to depend upon. Everyone at home has certainly been darn swell to me. Don't worry, mom, please because all of your boys will come back home safely, this war will be over soon. Some night we will all be together again & it will seem like everything was just a great big dream. At least no one can say that Mr. & Mrs. Niland's four sons were draft dodgers. Tell Eddie that I wish him the very best of luck. He will be O.K., in fact he will probably make the best soldier of the four of us. Ed will have a fine bunch of buddies by the sound of margaret's letter. Marvil, Inky, Eddie Steffans, a fine looking bunch of rookies they will be. I can see them now marching around and then I have a right to call them guys rookies. In the army now, they are called jeeps instead of rookies. But, seriously, I think those other guys won't be as good, but Eddie can go & keep up with the best of them.

I'll write him a letter the first chance that I get. I received muggsy's card, it was very nice of him to think of me. Thank marge for her letter too. My work around here is nothing really important to speak of. You see, mom, we are a field hospital and our work will come when we go into action somewhere. It will be quite awhile yet because they need more men before they can do anything. So as far as your no. 3 son goes he is in good hands and is feeling fine. As soon as you get Fritzs address send it to me I would like very much to write him. Pete is in San Francis, I hope he does alright for himself. He has certainly did a lot of traveling in the past year. A couple more like him in the army and the war would end quick.

2

Did Fritz have a good party the night before he left? Gosh, it is going to be tough keeping track of those brothers of mine. But we are a tough bunch aren't we, mom and we can take this thing in stride.

Mother, I miss you a terribly lot and I love you very dearly & deeply. When I do come back home to stay, I promise you that I will be a better man & a son that you can be truly proud of. The soldiers and clean-cut young men is because of the fine & decent way that you mom & Dad raised us. We have always been taught the right thing and because of you we have grown into good wholesome America's boys. I only hope that I can live up to the standards set by the rest of our family, on both sides we have always had the cleanest of service records. Dad came out with flying colors, and so will the rest of us. When they start handing out the praise, it should go to the mother & father like you & Dad who send their boys out in defense of their country.

I used to have some funny idea's and dreams about when I was younger. Down inside of me, mom, I'm still just the little baby next to Fritz, who used to be afraid of the dark and who always ran to his mother when he was in trouble. Honest, mom, that is what I always want to be, my mother's little baby boy, it will always be the way I feel. And even today if something happened I would find my mother and then I would be alright again. Well, I'll have to close now, mom, because it is getting late and the lights will be going out soon. Maybe I can come home one of these week-ends, I hope so. I think I'll have a good chance. Well, mom, keep your every night. I'm praying for the rest of the family. Give my love to Dad and the whole world for my father and the best mother in the world. My mom is a real lady. She is tops.

Your loving son,
Scotty

...all of your boys will come back

"Saving Private Ryan" was inspired by many stories of families who lost more than one boy during World War II. The Nilands of Tonawanda, New York, were such a family. Four Niland sons — Robert, Preston, Edward, and Frederick — served in the war. Edward's bomber went down over Burma on May 20, 1944, and, although he was presumed dead for more than a year, he was released from a prison camp in Rangoon on April 30, 1945, and survived the war. Frederick, a paratrooper in France, also survived, but the other two boys were not so fortunate. Preston died on June 6th, 1944, and Robert was killed the next day, D-Day, June 7th. The following letter was written by Robert (known as Bobby) shortly before he died.

Jan. 28, 1942

Dearest Mother:

How are you, Mom? I received your very nice letter & I was awfully glad to hear from you. I received all the letters of recommendation and my income tax check. Thank Dad for getting that stuff for me, I appreciate it very much. It is certainly swell to have a family like ours behind me, I know that I will always have someone to depend upon. Everyone at home has certainly been darn swell to me. Don't worry, Mom, please, because all of your boys will come back home safely, this war will be over soon. Some night we will all be together again & it will seem like everything was just a great big dream. At least no one can say that Mr. & Mrs. Niland's four sons were draft dodgers. Tell Eddie that I wish him the very best of luck. He will be O.K., in fact he will probably make the best soldier of the four of us. Ed will have a fine bunch of buddies by the sound

Letter left: Courtesy of the Niland family.

of Margaret's letter . . . a fine-looking bunch of
rookies they will be. I can see them now marching
around and the non-coms pushing the orders at
them. Boy, I would pay $1000 to see that. You
know, Mom, since my training period is over, now
I'm supposed to be a seasoned soldier. Therefore I
have a right to call them guys rookies. In the Army
now, they are called jeeps instead of rookies. But,
seriously, I think those other guys won't be so good,
but Eddie can go & keep up with the best of them.
I'll write him a letter the first chance that I get. I
received Muggsy's card, it was very nice of him to
think of me. Thank Marge for her letter too. My
work around here is nothing really important to
speak of. You see, Mom, we are a field hospital
and our work will come when we go into action
somewhere. It will be quite a while yet because they
need more men before they can do anything. So as
far as your no. 3 son goes, he is in good hands and is
feeling fine. As soon as you get Fritz's address, send
it to me. I would like very much to write him. Pete
in San Francisco, I hope he does alright for himself.
He has certainly done a lot of traveling in the past
year. A couple more like him in the Army and the
war would end quick. Did Fritz have a good party
the night before he left? Gosh, it is going to be
tough keeping track of those brothers of mine. But
we are a tough bunch, aren't we, Mom, and we
can take this thing in stride. Mother, I miss you a
terribly lot and I love you very dearly & deeply.
When I do come back home to stay, I promise you
that I will be a better man & a son that you can be
truly proud of. The reason us Niland boys are all
making good soldiers and clean-cut young men is

because of the fine & decent way that you & Dad raised us. We have always been taught the right thing and because of you we have grown into good wholesome American boys. I only hope that I can live up to the standards set by the rest of our family, on both sides we have always had the cleanest of service records. Uncle Fred and Dad came out with flying colors, and so will the rest of us. When they start handing out the praise, it should go to the mothers & fathers like you & Dad who send their boys out in defense of their country. Please, Mom, don't worry. Everything is going to turn out fine, just watch & pray & hope. You know, Mom, I try to make believe that I'm a big grown man & a soldier all dressed up. Just like I used to dream about when I was younger. Down inside of me, Mom, I'm still just the little baby next to Fritz, who used to be afraid of the dark and who always ran to his mother when he was in trouble. Honest, Mom, that is what I always want to be—my mother's little baby boy, it will always be the way I feel. And even today if something happened I would find my mother and then I would be alright again. Well, I'll have to close now, Mom, because it is getting late and the lights will be going out soon. Maybe I can come home one of these week-ends. I hope so. I think I'll have a good chance. Well, Mom, keep that old chin of yours up & I'm praying for you every night. Give my love to Dad and the rest of the family. I have the best guy in the whole world for my father and the best mother in the world. My mom is a real lady. She is tops.

Your loving son
Bobby

Part Eight

"A Journal of Personal Reactions"

Overleaf photo: Private First Class Francis M. Lee (left), U.S. Army; First Lieutenant Thomas P. Lee (right), U.S. Army; Milan, Italy, circa 1945. Courtesy of Joan Lee Murray.

Inset photo: Staff Sergeant Andrew MacDonald (left), U.S. Marines, 5th Division; Petty Officer, 3rd Class, Donald MacDonald (right), U.S.N.R.; Hawaii, circa 1945. Courtesy of Mina Chisholm Kennedy.

A Journal of Personal Reactions

Please use these pages to express your own feelings and opinions about "Saving Private Ryan" and your reactions to these e-mail messages. This is your space to write whatever is in your heart.

Acknowledgments

Many people contributed to making this book possible. First and foremost, the many thousands of people who bared their feelings in messages posted on the AOL site. These "letters" inspired us to conceive and publish a book that would be a remembrance, not just for the contributors, but for everyone who was touched by the remarkable movie *Saving Private Ryan*.

We want to thank all the contributors of messages, and of the historical photos. Also, Jesse Kornbluth, Editorial Director of Channel Programming for America Online, and editor Linda Sunshine, who so well managed the daunting task of reviewing and organizing the selections with such care and respect; Timothy Shaner, for his talented design; Harry Burton, John Cook, Frank DeMaio, Nancy Kenney, and Ann Lee of Newmarket Press who helped to make all the pieces fit together; and the following people at DreamWorks and America Online, especially Steven Spielberg, Steve Case, and Bob Pittman, who believed in this idea and encouraged their staffs to make this book happen.

At America Online: Ann Brackbill, Jim Bramson, Kathy Bushkin, Alan Feldenkris, Jennifer Fiore, Wendy Goldberg, Chris Johnson, Kathy Johnson, Kathy Lentz, Lisa McCabe, Esther McCullough, Pam McGraw, Jennifer Maffett, Miguel Monteverde, Debbie Perkins, Heather Perram, Phil Rappoport, Pavia Rosati, Colette Rhoney, Cindy Royce, Margaret Ryan, Jonathan Sacks, Jason Seiken, Andrea Spiegel, Kate Tipul, Helen Vance, and Nancy Whalen.

At DreamWorks: Bonnie Curtis, Kristy Cox, Paul Elliott, Brad Globe, Garrett Lawson, Marvin Levy, Anne McGrath, Randy Nellis, Michele Oakes, Mark Russell, Dorit Saines, Jerry Schmitz, and Zoe Shepherd.

— Esther Margolis, President & Publisher, Newmarket Press